PETRA
and the LOST KINGDOM
of the NABATAEANS

PETRA
and the LOST KINGDOM
of the NABATAEANS

Jane Taylor

Harvard University Press

Cambridge, Massachusetts

2002

For David and Anna
With love and gratitude

Copyright © Jane Taylor, 2001

Published in the United Kingdom in 2001 by I.B. Tauris & Co Ltd

ISBN 0-674-00849-9

A full CIP record for this book is available from the Library of Congress

Designed and typeset in Centaur by Karen Stafford, London
Printed and bound in Spain

The publishers wish to thank the following for their generous support in the publication of this book:

Union Bank
Business Tourism Company
Jordan National Bank
Nuqul Group
Agricultural Materials Company
Greater Amman Municipality
Hotel Inter-Continental Jordan
Jordan Telecom
Grand Hyatt Amman
GHQ Jordan Armed Forces
Specialized Investment Compounds Company
Arab International Hotels Company
El-Zay Ready Wear Manufacturing Company
Standard Chartered Grindlays Bank
International Data Exchange (INDEX)
Central Bank of Jordan
Export and Finance Bank
INT@J, Information Technology Association - Jordan
National Equipment and Technical Services (NETS)
JWICO – Jordan Wood Industries Company
Ammon Shipping & Transport
Ideal Group
CDC – Communications Development Company
Hikma Pharmaceuticals

CONTENTS

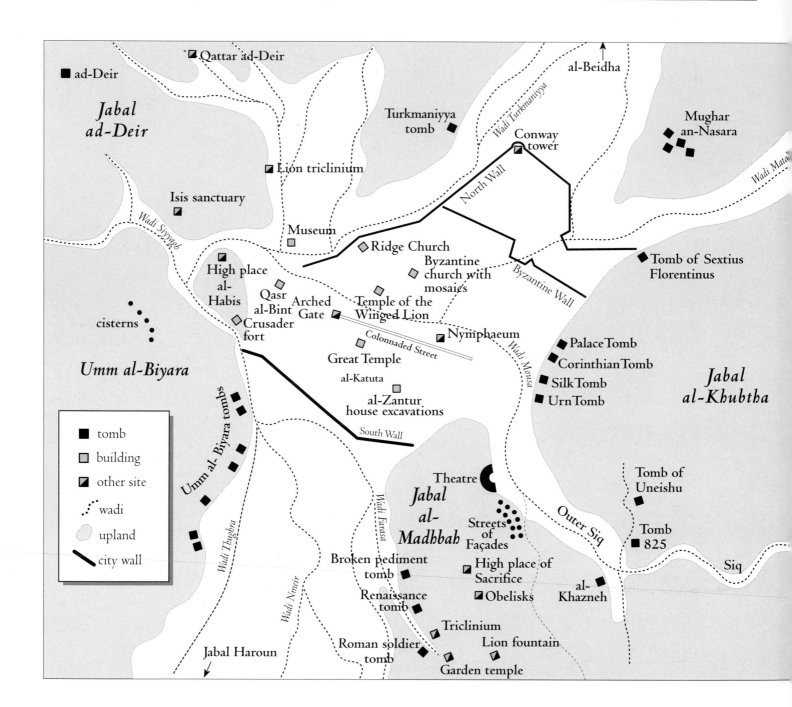

■ ad-Deir

■ Qattar ad-Deir

Jabal ad-Deir

Turkmaniyya tomb

al-Beidha

Wadi Turkmaniyya

Conway tower

Mughar an-Nasara

Wadi Mata

▨ Lion triclinium

North Wall

Isis sanctuary ▨

Wadi Siyyagh

Museum

◆ Ridge Church

Byzantine church with mosaics

Byzantine Wall

◆ Tomb of Sextius Florentinus

High place al-Habis ▨

Qasr al-Bint

Arched Gate

Temple of the Winged Lion

Crusader fort ◆

Colonnaded Street

Nymphaeum

Wadi Mousa

■ Palace Tomb

cisterns

Umm al-Biyara

Great Temple

al-Katuta

■ Corinthian Tomb

■ Silk Tomb

■ Urn Tomb

Jabal al-Khubtha

al-Zantur house excavations

South Wall

Umm al-Biyara tombs

■	tomb
▢	building
▨	other site
⋯	wadi
	upland
▬	city wall

Wadi Thugbra

Wadi Farasa

Theatre

Jabal al-Madhbah

Streets of Façades

Outer Siq

Tomb of Uneishu

Tomb 825

Siq

Broken pediment tomb

High place of Sacrifice ▨

al-Khazneh

Wadi Nmeir

Renaissance tomb

▨ Obelisks

Jabal Haroun

Roman soldier tomb

Triclinium

Lion fountain

Garden temple

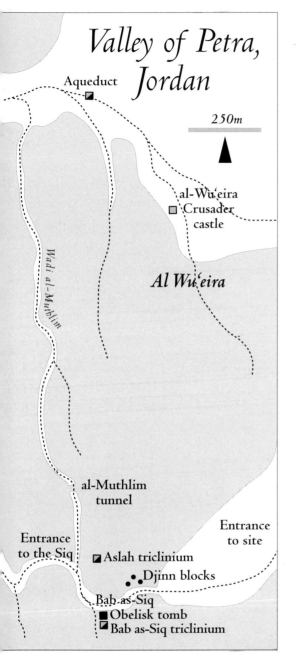

Valley of Petra, Jordan

250m

Aqueduct

al-Wu'eira Crusader castle

Al Wu'eira

Wadi al-Muthlim

al-Muthlim tunnel

Entrance to the Siq

Entrance to site

Aslah triclinium

Djinn blocks

Bab as-Siq
Obelisk tomb
Bab as-Siq triclinium

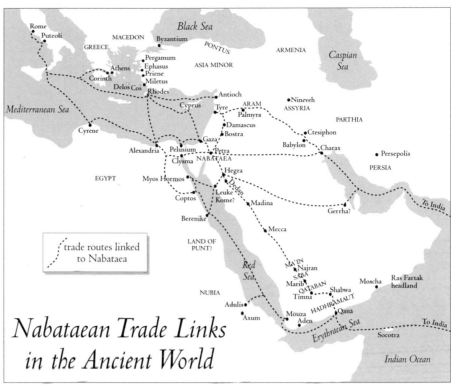

Nabataean Trade Links in the Ancient World

Rome
Puteoli
GREECE
MACEDON
Black Sea
Byzantium
PONTUS
ARMENIA
Caspian Sea
Pergamum
Ephasus
Priene
Miletus
ASIA MINOR
Athens
Corinth
Delos Cos
Rhodes
Antioch
Nineveh
ASSYRIA
PARTHIA
Mediterranean Sea
Cyprus
Tyre
ARAM
Palmyra
Damascus
Bostra
Ctesiphon
Babylon
Charax
Persepolis
PERSIA
Cyrene
Gaza
Alexandria
Pelusium
Petra
Clysma
NABATAEA
EGYPT
Myos Hormos
Hegra
Dedan
To India
Coptos
Leuke Kome?
Madina
Gerrha?
Berenike
Mecca
trade routes linked to Nabataea
LAND OF PUNT?
Red Sea
MA'IN
Najran
SABA
Marib
Moscha
Ras Fartak headland
NUBIA
QATABAN
Timna
Shabwa
HADHRAMAUT
Adulis
Mouza
Aden
Qana
Axum
Erythraean Sea
To India
Socotra
Indian Ocean

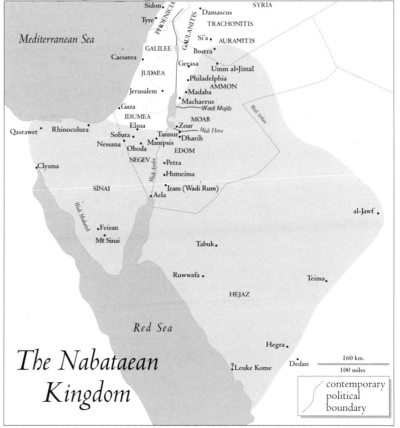

The Nabataean Kingdom

Sidon
PHOENICIA
Damascus
SYRIA
Tyre
TRACHONITIS
GAULANITIS
Si'a
AURANITIS
Mediterranean Sea
GALILEE
Bostra
Caesarea
Gerasa
Umm al-Jimal
JUDAEA
Philadelphia
AMMON
Jerusalem
Madaba
Machaerus
Wadi Mujib
Gaza
IDUMEA
Elusa
MOAB
Zoar
Wadi Sillan
Qasrawet
Rhinocolura
Sobata
Tannur
Wadi Hasa
Nessana
Mampsis
Dharih
Oboda
EDOM
Clysma
NEGEV
Petra
Wadi Araba
Humeima
SINAI
Iram (Wadi Rum)
Wadi Mukatteb
Aela
al-Jawf
Feiran
Mt Sinai
Tabuk
Ruwwafa
Teima
HEJAZ
Red Sea
Hegra
Dedan
?Leuke Kome
160 km.
100 miles
contemporary political boundary

PREFACE

O F ALL THE POWERFUL, rich and gifted peoples of the ancient world, the Nabataeans are the most unjustly forgotten. They deserve to be better known – as Alexander the Great, Pompey, Julius Caesar, King Herod, Cleopatra, Mark Antony, the Emperor Augustus, John the Baptist, the apostle Paul and a starry crowd of other contemporaries could ruefully confirm. They may seem improbable candidates for such recognition: once nomads, ever on the move with their flocks and herds, by the middle of the first millennium BC they had found a new focus for their wanderings by trading in precious frankincense, myrrh and spices, and they became wealthy. They extended their control over the rich trade routes of the Middle East, operating a mixed economy of direct trade and the provision of travel services and protection for merchants from other lands.

Yet, by the second century BC, the Nabataeans had established a kingdom whose heartland was in present-day Jordan, and which controlled a wide area from northern Arabia in the south to Syria in the north, from Sinai and the Negev in the west to Wadi Sirhan and al-Jawf in the east. The Nabataean kingdom was considered one of the major players in the Mediterranean world, and the people were famed and envied for their vast wealth, the strength and independence of their state, their good governance and their skills in trade, hydraulic engineering and the arts. Supremely, the Nabataeans were renowned for their spectacular rock-cut city, Petra, a legend in its own time – as it still is today.

The story of the Nabataeans has as many omissions as certainties. Faced with the slenderness of their own records, we grasp at legends on coins, inscriptions in stone and a handful of papyrus archives. Then there are the outside sources – tantalizingly incomplete references by contemporaries of other nationalities, sometimes admiring, often critical, always partisan – each casting light on a small area of the life of these fascinating people who recurrently preoccupied their neighbours, friends and foes alike. From the classical world we have Herodotus, Hieronymus of Cardia, Diodorus of Sicily, Strabo, Pliny the Elder, Dio Cassius, Plutarch, the anonymous author of the *Periplus of the Erythraean Sea*, and Flavius Josephus; from the Byzantine period, Jerome, Justin, Procopius, Stephen of Byzantium, Ouranios and Photius; and there are a few ambiguous references from early Islamic writers.

The quest for peace in the Middle East has brought a sharp rise in interest in this crucial area of the world, and in its peoples, past and present. Many places where the Nabataeans once ruled are now, for the first time in half a century, mutually accessible; they are strikingly beautiful in their natural landscape, and fascinating for the wealth of their monuments. Many people who until only recently had never heard of Petra, let alone of the Nabataeans, are now beginning to wonder about the people who created one of the most astonishing sites of the ancient world.

This book is an attempt to bring this brilliant but neglected people, long known to scholars, into a wider beam of light 2000 years after their heyday. I have no pretensions to original scholarship but have tried to assimilate something of the fascinating work of those who have been at the sharp end of archaeological and historical research. Information about the Nabataeans has so far only been found in a range of academic books and articles, and in archaeologists' excavation reports – these I have joyously plundered for some of the gems of knowledge and inspirational guesswork that they contain. Most rewarding of all are the original documents that have been discovered in recent years, and I have been constantly delighted by revelations of common human passions, sympathies, quirks and foibles in some of those ancient characters who have become known to me as I read their letters or law suits. I have written as I have read, with shameless self-indulgence, trying always to imagine what it might have been like to have been there in Petra, or Gaza, or Sinai, or Jerusalem, with the Nabataeans and the people with whom they had dealings two millennia ago.

My greatest debt of gratitude is to His Majesty the late King Hussein, who encouraged me at the beginning of my work on the Nabataeans, at the time when peace between Jordan and Israel was still in the process of being brokered. I called it my 'peace plan' book; but for too long since then the prospects for King Hussein's dream of a comprehensive peace in the Middle East have seemed dim. It is my deepest hope that people will soon be able to travel as freely as the Nabataeans did between the various parts of their erstwhile lands. I have been fortunate to be able to travel more freely than many, thanks to the enormous privilege of living in Amman, the capital of the Hashemite Kingdom of Jordan, and so close to the centre of the Nabataeans' world.

It is thanks primarily to HM King Hussein, but also to HRH Prince Faisal bin al-Hussein, Brigadier Ziyad Hanandeh and the officers and pilots of the helicopter squadron of the Royal Jordanian Air Force, that I have been fortunate enough to photograph many of these sites from the air. I am very conscious of, and grateful for, these privileged opportunities that I have been given.

I have received much help from many scholars who have been extraordinarily generous and patient in sharing their knowledge and insights in their various areas of expertise. Each chapter, as it came off the computer, was first sent to Dr Piotr Bienkowski, Curator of Egyptian and Near Eastern Antiquities at the Liverpool Museum and a specialist in the Edomites, whose sharp eye and kind pen softened the ordeal of the first exposure of my infant text. When he passed a chapter as generally sound I then had the courage to send it to other scholars – specialists in various fields of Nabataean studies – for further vetting. Those who kindly agreed to be subjected to this task, or who provided abundant information, were: the perennially generous Professor Martha Sharp Joukowsky of Brown University, Rhode Island; Dr Fawzi Zayadine, then Deputy Director of the Department of Antiquities in Amman; Michael Macdonald of the Oriental Institute, University of Oxford; Peter Parr of the Institute of Archaeology, University of London; Professor John Healey of the University of Manchester; Dr François Villeneuve of the Ecole normale supérieure, Paris; Professor David Graf, University of Miami, Professor Hannah Cotton of the Hebrew University, Jerusalem; Baruch Levine, Skirball Professor of Bible and Ancient Near Eastern Studies at New York University; Dr Robert Schick and Avner Goren, both of the W. F. Albright Institute of Archaeological Research, Jerusalem; Professors Jaakko Frösén and Maarit Kaimio of the University of Helsinki; Professor Ludwig Koenen of the University of Michigan; Dr Robert Daniel (part of the Michigan team on the Petra papyri); and Dr Patricia Bikai of the American Center of Oriental Research, Amman. All were unfailingly generous in their detailed comments and suggestions.

When all the chapters had been put into semi-final shape, John Julius Norwich, fine and supremely readable historian that he is, heroically agreed to read the whole typescript. So too did Professor Glen Bowersock of the Institute for Advanced Study, Princeton, doyen of Nabataean/Roman studies, whose further suggestions illuminated yet more fascinating aspects of this prodigiously gifted Arab people. Dr Ghazi Bisheh, erstwhile Director General of the Department of Antiquities of the Ministry of Tourism of Jordan also read and commented on the complete text, as did Dr Fawzi Zayadine (some chapters for the second time). Their deep knowledge respectively of the late-Byzantine to early-Islamic periods, and of the whole Nabataean story, clarified several ambiguities for me.

To all of you my heartfelt gratitude for preventing, or reducing, my worst errors and inconsistencies. Those that remain are all my own.

In addition, Alan and Brigid Waddams, with characteristic generosity, not only introduced me to Nabataean sites in the Hauran in southern Syria, but also looked after me on numerous occasions in their oasis of a house in Damascus. Tommy Leitersdorf, then Chairman of the Negev Tourism Development Administration, twice sent me with all possible support and help to see Nabataean sites in the Negev, on the first occasion accompanied (with infectious enthusiasm) by Yadin Roman and Dita Kohl of *Eretz Magazine*. James Watt, lately of the British Embassy, Amman, masterminded an unforgettable expedition to enable me to see Meda'in Saleh, the magnificent Nabataean site in the Hejaz region of Saudi Arabia. Avner Goren included me in a trip to the Sinai to look at Nabataean inscriptions – for 15 years he had been in charge of archaeology in the Sinai and, even after the more than 20 years since he left, the bedouin of the region still love him. It was a rare privilege to travel with him. While in the Sinai, Dr John Grainger, Project Manager of the St Katherine Protectorate, gave me generous help and hospitality. Eli Raz of Ein Gedi offered some of his precious time and expertise to take me climbing one golden day among the cliffs and caves of Nahal Hever, so that I could see where the remarkable Babatha spent her last days nearly 2000 years ago. Professor Tom Paradise, of the University of Arkansas, Fayetteville, with his usual large-heartedness offered to make the maps for the book. Dr Derek Roebuck, from his current research for a series of books on the history of arbitration, provided some invaluable information on the subject; he and his writer wife, Susanna Hoe, have always generously given me moral and practical support, and hospitality, when I most needed it. And I am blessed with a supportive, patient and vigilant literary agent, and friend, Sara Mengüç.

On my visits to London my brother and sister-in-law, David and Anna Taylor, have been unfailingly and abundantly hospitable, often for longer stretches than most human patience could handle. So too has William Taylor, whose Ealing vicarage, for the eight years he was there, constantly teemed with his friends from all around the globe.

My frequent sorties to Petra from my home in Amman are always enriched by time spent with my friends of the Bdoul bedouin tribe – in particular Mohammed and Marguerite, whose home is my own second home; Dakhilallah Qublan, who has taught me so much about the workings of Petra and the Nabataeans, and his wife Rakhiyah; and Awadh Salameh, who has taken me on foot or camelback along ancient Nabataean routes out of Petra and into Wadi Araba. I am grateful for, and deeply touched by, their friendship and hospitality, as also that of Haroun and Lidia, and many more of the Bdoul.

My warmest and most abundant thanks to you all.

Photographic note

The films for this book were generously sponsored by Fujifilm, Jordan – for which I am particularly grateful since I have for several years had a love-affair with Fujichrome Velvia and Fujichrome Provia. Their glowing tones and fine grain are, in my opinion, unmatched by any other film. The cameras I use are a Pentax 6x7 medium format camera, with 90mm and 45mm lenses; and, for 35mm cameras, Nikon FE and FE2, with a range of Nikkor lenses from 20mm to 200mm – all trusty old workhorses.

PRELUDE

Alexander the Great, Frankincense and the Nabataeans

WHEN ALEXANDER THE GREAT was a boy in Macedon, his curmudgeonly tutor once caught him scooping handfuls of precious frankincense to burn on the altar as an abundant offering to the gods. Leonidas clucked reprovingly.

'Alexander, when you have conquered the lands which produce these aromatics, then you can scatter incense in this extravagant manner. Until then, don't waste it.'

The young prince stored the rebuke away in his memory.

Twenty years later Alexander captured Gaza on the eastern Mediterranean coast after a long, hard siege. It was a great port then, entrepôt for most of the trading goods brought from the east for shipping to Europe – including Macedon. When the Macedonians entered the city they discovered vast stores of incense and spices which merchants had brought overland by camel caravan from southern Arabia. From these rich reserves Alexander sent the now elderly Leonidas a gift of 500 talents (13.7 tonnes) of frankincense and 100 talents of myrrh.

He also sent a message: 'I have sent you frankincense and myrrh in abundance, to stop you being stingy towards the gods.'[1]

It was not only a humorous and pointed reproof to a mean old man; it was a clear statement that, if Alexander had not yet conquered the lands of southern Arabia which produced these aromatics, he was at least halfway there. At such a victorious moment in his life the achievement of the other half of that challenge may have seemed inevitable.

What if Alexander's attendant seer had chosen that moment to venture a prophecy that within two centuries the tribe of nomads who had brought the frankincense and myrrh on the final long stage of their journey to Gaza would control a large part of the lands that Alexander had conquered in the Middle East? Would Alexander have dismissed him as a dreamer? Yet he of all men should have understood the capacity of gifted

ALEXANDER THE GREAT, WHEN HE CAPTURED THE GREAT PORT OF GAZA, SENT HIS CHILDHOOD TUTOR IN MACEDON SEVERAL TONNES OF FRANKINCENSE AND MYRRH FROM THE VAST RESERVES HE FOUND STORED THERE. THEY HAD BEEN BROUGHT FROM ARABIA BY THE NABATAEANS, WHO CONTROLLED THE LAST STRETCH OF THE TRADE ROUTE, FROM THE NORTH-WEST ARABIAN PENINSULA TO THE MEDITERRANEAN. (ISTANBUL ARCHAEOLOGICAL MUSEUM.)

THE MEDITERRANEAN COAST AT GAZA TODAY. FROM HERE INCENSE AND SPICES WERE SHIPPED TO EUROPE FOR USE IN RELIGIOUS RITUALS, MEDICINE, PRESERVING FOOD, KEEPING INSECTS AT BAY, AND MASKING NOXIOUS ODOURS.

human beings to change – first themselves, then their surroundings. And he may already have seen the tell-tale signs of genius of this particular tribe of nomads.

One of his officers, Hieronymus of Cardia, did see the signs, and was impressed enough to write about these 'barbarians' in some detail. He noted their wealth, derived from trade in frankincense, myrrh and other spices which they brought from Arabia to Gaza to ship to Europe. He saw their ability to collect and store water in the uncompromising desert, and understood that this enabled them to elude adversaries less desert-wise than themselves; thus they remained free. This ability also enabled them to cross long stretches of arid terrain that was inaccessible to others, and so cut vital days off the journeys of their trading caravans; thus they increased their wealth.

Alexander had not reached the source of these precious aromatics and, despite his later plans to do so, he never did. But he had brushed with the people who were already in control of the most northerly part of the incense route.

They were the Nabataeans.

ONE

THEY CAME FROM ARABIA

The Origins of the Nabataeans
and the Incense Trade

A GROUP OF BEDOUIN FOLLOW AN OLD NABATAEAN ROUTE IN THE DESERT BETWEEN WADI ARABA AND PETRA. EVEN THE STEEPEST SLOPES COULD BE NEGOTIATED BY BUILDING A PATH IN A SUCCESSION OF LONG ZIGZAGS.

S OMEWHERE IN THE VAST reaches of Arabia, in the centuries before Alexander the Great, the Nabataeans moved with their flocks and herds, finding grazing and water where they could. They followed well worn routes as season succeeded season, staying in familiar camping grounds while conditions were good in that area; then, as the supply of food for themselves and their animals diminished, they moved on to other places where long usage told them they would again find pasture and water. In bad years, when the expected seasonal rains did not fall, even the oases would quickly be stripped of grazing, and life was reduced to a day-by-day, hour-by-hour quest for survival.

The Nabataeans were simply one among many nomadic tribes, most of whom sank without trace in the anonymity that had always encompassed them. But this tribe was different: they emerged into the beam of history and prospered abundantly during their episode in the light, before fading again into the shadows.

The precise origins of the Nabataeans remain as hazy as a desert sandstorm, despite a handful of hypotheses of varying degrees of persuasiveness. While virtually all scholars agree that they were Arabs, some have argued that they came from the south-west of the Arabian peninsula, today's Yemen; yet their language, their script and their gods have nothing in common with those of southern Arabia. An alternative theory locates their original home on the east coast of the peninsula, opposite Bahrain, where they certainly had trading links. More convincing is the suggestion that they were from the north-west, in today's Hejaz region of Saudi Arabia, for they share several deities with the ancient people there, and the root consonants of their tribal name — *nbtw* — are found in early Semitic languages from this region.

There are also indications that they may have come from Mesopotamia. Twice in the eighth century BC, in the annals of two Assyrian kings, a tribe called the Nabatu is listed as one of many rebellious Arab groups in the region. By the next century a communications route ran between the northern ends of the Gulf and the Red Sea; and similarities between what is known of the Arabic dialect of Mesopotamia in the Neo-Assyrian period and the later Nabataean Arabic suggest that there may have been a connection between the two. The Nabataeans may have originated in Mesopotamia, migrated westwards between the sixth and fourth centuries BC, and settled in north-west Arabia and much of what is now Jordan.[1]

Assyrian annals of the mid-seventh century BC tell of King Ashurbanipal, among his many conquests, defeating a people called the 'Nabaiati', who lived 'in a far off desert place where there are no wild animals and not even the birds build their nests'. But the temptation to link the Nabaiati with the Nabataeans because of the similarity of their names is rejected by most scholars — the Semitic name of the Nabataeans, *nbtw*, differs from that of the Nabaiati, *nbyt*, in the two final consonants. The Nabaiati are generally identified with the Nebaioth of the Bible[2], who took the name of their supposed forebear, the eldest son of Ishmael, son of Abraham; they too have sometimes been mistakenly identified with the Nabataeans.

'THEY LIVE IN THE OPEN AIR, CLAIMING AS NATIVE LAND A WILDERNESS THAT HAS NEITHER RIVERS NOR ABUNDANT SPRINGS... SOME OF THEM RAISE CAMELS, OTHERS SHEEP, PASTURING THEM IN THE DESERT'. DOUBTLESS THEY ALSO RAISED GOATS, FROM WHOSE HAIR BLACK TENT CLOTH HAS ALWAYS BEEN MADE.

THE NARROW MOUTH OF ONE OF MANY LARGE CISTERNS ON THE GREAT ROCK OF UMM AL-BIYARA THAT OVERLOOKS PETRA. A SYSTEM OF CHANNELS DIRECTED WATER INTO THE CISTERNS WHICH WERE LINED WITH STUCCO, SOME OF WHICH CAN STILL BE SEEN. CISTERNS SUCH AS THIS ENABLED THE NABATAEANS TO SURVIVE IN AREAS THAT WERE TOO ARID FOR OTHER NOMADS.

The first secure historical reference to this elusive people comes from the Greek historian, Diodorus of Sicily, who, although he wrote in the late first century BC, included informa-tion about the Nabataeans of some 300 years earlier. His source was one of Alexander the Great's officers, Hieronymus of Cardia, who had had first-hand experience of them. He portrays a tribe of pastoralist nomads who observed uncompromising rules, and lived off their herds and the edible plants that grew wild around them:

> [They] range over a country which is partly desert and partly waterless, though a small section of it is fruitful… They live in the open air, claiming as native land a wilder-

ness that has neither rivers nor abundant springs… It is their custom neither to plant grain, set out any fruit-bearing tree, use wine, nor construct any house; and if anyone is found acting contrary to this, death is his penalty… Some of them raise camels, others sheep, pasturing them in the desert… They themselves use as food flesh and milk and those of the plants that grow from the ground that are suitable for this purpose.[3]

But this is only part of the picture. The reason for the Nabataeans' austere lifestyle, and for the draconian penalty against nonconformists, was doubtless that agriculture and immovable possessions such as houses or stocks of wine would hamper the tribe's ability to evaporate into the thin desert air when threatened by enemies – it was vital that they leave nothing that could be destroyed or spoiled. The one thing in which the Nabataeans had superior expertise over more sophisticated adversaries was their knowledge of the desert; they knew its every feature and refuge, and in it they had cunningly dug out large underground cisterns, undetectable to the inexpert eye:

whenever a strong force of enemies comes near, they take refuge in the desert, using this as a fortress; for it lacks water and cannot be crossed by others, but to them alone, since they have prepared subterranean reservoirs lined with stucco, it furnishes safety… they make great excavations…, the mouths of which they make very small, but by constantly increasing the width as they dig deeper, they make them of such size that each side has the length of one plethrum [30 metres]. After filling these reservoirs with rain water, they close the openings, making them even with the rest of the ground, and they leave signs that are known to themselves but are unrecognizable to others.[4]

The Nabataeans had found that control of water facilitated freedom of movement and, wrote Diodorus, they were 'exceptionally fond of freedom'. Secrecy was necessary to guard this freedom, though the Greeks must have discovered at least one Nabataean reservoir to allow such a precise description. This mastery of the desert had enabled the Nabataeans to maintain their liberty even when threatened by awe-inspiring enemies, for 'neither the Assyrians of old, nor the kings of the Medes and Persians, nor yet those of the Macedonians have been able to enslave them, and… they never brought their attempts to a successful conclusion'.

The Nabataeans had also discovered another source of freedom – wealth – and this, too, distinguished them from other contemporary Arab tribes of the desert. Their main source of wealth may seem surprising for nomads – trade. 'Not a few of them', wrote Diodorus/Hieronymus,[5] 'are accustomed to bring down to the [Mediterranean] sea frankincense and myrrh and the most valuable kinds of spices, which they procure from those who convey them from what is called Eudaimon Arabia' (in today's Yemen). But trade was a logical extension of their nomadic life for it implemented all their mastery of desert conditions; it gave a new and profitable focus to their wanderings.

Few peoples have made so dramatic a metamorphosis from a harsh pastoral and nomadic existence, with a little trade on the side, to a settled life in fine cities, commanding an extensive trading empire. Within two or three centuries the Nabataeans became the shrewdest of traders, ingenious hydraulic engineers and productive farmers, and acquired legendary wealth. They created carved façades and buildings of extraordinary architectural beauty and originality that were a wonder in their own time, and they produced some of the most exquisite pottery of the ancient world. It is unlikely that in so short a time they could have sprung fully formed from such primitive and precarious beginnings by their own unaided efforts. Even recognizing their genius offers insufficient explanation for so swift an evolution to such sophistication of mind and technology. Their rare gift was to learn from the skills of others, and to transform disparate ideas into something uniquely their own.

In the centuries that the Nabataeans moved through Arabia, they were in contact with many tribes, some nomadic like themselves, others in settled farming communities. A very few, like the people of Saba, Ma'in, Qataban and Hadhramaut (today in Yemen), by the sixth and fifth centuries BC were spectacularly advanced in architecture and water technology, and wealthy both from their abundant agriculture and from trade in frankincense and myrrh. The south Arabians had doubtless learned many skills from the even more advanced people of Mesopotamia; but the incense trade was all their own. So great was their wealth believed to be that the early Greeks, on the unphilosophical premise that wealth equals felicity, enviously referred to the whole of south-west Arabia as Eudaimon (blessed) Arabia. Later the Romans, equally impressed and envious, translated the epithet into Latin – *Arabia Felix*. Nowhere else in the Arabian peninsula did such riches and technology exist together. It was also the starting point of the incense route. This

In the second half of the eighth century BC there is firmer evidence of these people. At this time the industrious scribes of a succession of Assyrian kings recorded that Tiglath-pileser III was sent tribute of gold, camels and spices by 'the Sabaeans'. The first reference to a ruler is in 715 BC when even richer tribute was sent to Sargon II by 'Yith'amar, ruler of Saba', followed some 30 years later by gifts to Sennacherib from another ruler called Karib'il. The word 'spices' included a wide variety of aromatics, but for those early Sabaeans their home-grown spices were the highly prized frankincense and myrrh.

At Marib, capital of the Sabaean kingdom, square columns tower above the remains of what may have been a palace. Dating from at least the seventh century BC, Arsh Bilqis (throne of Bilqis – the name in the Koran for the Queen of Sheba) today provides a fine climbing ground for local lads.

THE SOUTHERN SLUICE OF THE GREAT MARIB DAM, WHICH WAS CONNECTED BY A BARRAGE WALL TO THE NORTHERN SLUICE ON THE OTHER SIDE OF THE WADI. THE DAM CREATED AN AGRICULTURAL REVOLUTION FOR THE SABAEAN PEOPLE FROM PERHAPS AS EARLY AS THE EIGHTH CENTURY BC; IT SILTED UP FREQUENTLY, AND BROKE FOR THE LAST TIME IN THE EARLY SEVENTH CENTURY AD.

By the sixth century BC Saba was ruled by hereditary priest-kings called *mukarribs*, 'covenant-makers', and it is they who built the first durable Sabaean monuments. The south Arabians had mastered the techniques of quarrying and transporting large blocks of stone; and their skilled masons, using simple chisels, shaped and smoothed the stones with which their architects created monuments of great beauty and grandeur. The vast Marib dam, and the magnificent temples for the worship of their gods, built both at Marib and elsewhere in the Sabaean kingdom, reflect the blend of practical and spiritual aspirations of the gifted *mukarribs* of the day — gods and water dominated their lives. The two stone-built sluices of the ancient dam still stand, but the 750-metre stone-faced earth wall of the dam itself, so often repaired during its millennium of service, is now reduced to a few sections. It was a miracle of engineering — the great, curved barrage wall, stretching across the flood bed of Wadi Dhana, held back the water that accumulated during the rainy season, while the sluice gates, like the valves of an enormous aqueous heart, sent it along raised canals to distribution points, then through an intricate network of irrigation channels to the fields. At carefully regulated intervals throughout each day, this complex system of hydraulic arteries watered a vast area — around 72 square km — of fertile agricultural land.

The ancient dam produced a green revolution. Sabaean agriculture was no longer afflicted by the long seasons when no rain fell, and the arid heartland of the kingdom became richly productive. Agriculture, even more than the incense trade, underpinned the prosperity of ancient Saba for, while only a few Sabaeans dealt in aromatics, the great majority of the population was involved in agriculture — and agriculture depended on the efficient control of water. It was just this combination of skills, applied to similarly arid terrain, that the Nabataeans were to put to good use a few centuries later. For them, as for the Sabaeans, the gods and water were of supreme importance.

The Sabaeans were early operators in the trade in frankincense and myrrh, and in the sixth century BC probably also controlled most of the lands where they grew. The quantities were staggering: if Herodotus is to be believed, the 'Arabians' sent an annual tribute of 1000 talents (over 27 tonnes) of frankincense to Darius I of Persia who then controlled most of Arabia.

After about 400 BC Sabaean power slipped and Hadhramaut, Ma'in and Qataban became independent kingdoms. Myrrh grew over a wide area of southern Arabia, and especially in Qataban; but the kingdom of Hadhramaut, well to the east of Saba, was the only source of frankincense in the whole of Arabia from the fourth to first centuries BC. Though frankincense still grew along the east coast of Africa, the most highly prized (and priced) variety came from Hadhramaut alone, which then included Dhofar, now in Oman, and the island of Socotra in the Indian Ocean. So jealously did the south Arabians guard their frankincense production, that they spread colourful tales about the dangers of collecting it. Herodotus fell for one about flying snakes which were, he wrote:

> small in size and of various colours, and great numbers of them keep guard over all the trees which bear frankincense, and the only way to get rid of them is by smoking them out with storax. The Arabians say that the whole world would swarm with these creatures were it not for one peculiar fact — ... when they couple, the female seizes the male by the neck at the very moment of the release of the sperm, and hangs on until she has bitten it through. That finishes the male; and the female, too, has to pay for her behaviour, for the young in her belly avenge their father by gnawing at her insides, until they end by eating their way out.[7]

Tales about snakes infesting the frankincense forests persisted for several centuries, and were repeated in various forms by many of the ancient writers. Agatharchides of Cnidus, whose second century BC account was regurgitated by several later writers, declared that the 'most fragrant forests' swarmed with dark-red, leaping snakes, a span in length, whose bites were incurable if inflicted above the thigh. Lest we dismiss such stories as vivid invention, leaping red snakes with fatal bites have been reported in Hadhramaut in the twentieth century.[8]

These cautionary tales were probably for the consumption of the majority of Greeks who came by sea on their fact-finding missions. By land there would have been less need for deterring would-be intruders, for there were pitiless deserts to prevent most travellers from reaching the frankincense-growing areas. The ploy seems to have been successful, for the early Greek writers show a marked vagueness, and often a lack of accuracy, in their descriptions of what the frankincense and myrrh trees looked like, where and how they grew, and how their gum resins were harvested and traded. This was partly because the trees did not grow close to the sea, but inland. Only great courage or desperate need pushed some sailors to risk penetrating the interior of Arabia with its well publicized terrors.

It must have been frustrating for the scholarly botanist Theophrastus, Aristotle's most gifted pupil, to have to rely on second-hand reports by non-experts, or even sheer invention, on the nature of frankincense and myrrh trees. In his *Enquiry into Plants*,[9] written around 300 BC, his main informants were Greek sailors from the expedition sent by Alexander the Great. Afflicted by thirst, they had landed to look for water, but not finding any near the coast they had ventured inland to the mountains where they 'saw these trees and the manner of collecting their gums'. We sense his moral outrage when he writes of the sailors taking advantage of the local people who 'are honest in their dealings with each other. Wherefore no one keeps watch; so that these sailors greedily took... and put on board their ships some of the frankincense and myrrh, since there was no one about, and sailed away.'

The sailors' description of the frankincense tree – 'about five cubits high [2.3 metres], and it is much branched; it has a leaf like that of a pear, but much smaller and very grassy in colour, like rue; the bark is altogether smooth like that of a bay' – was accurate for the Arabian frankincense tree (*Boswellia sacra*), though Theophrastus had no means of checking. From the briefest of trunks grow several branches with ash-coloured, scaly bark, each branch dividing and growing outwards and upwards like a shrub to a height of 2 to 3 metres, dotted with tiny leaves. Frankincense used to grow abundantly throughout Hadhramaut and Dhofar, both in the hinterland and along the coast; today very few trees are found in western Hadhramaut, though more survive in Dhofar and on the island of Socotra.

Myrrh trees (*Commifora myrrha*) grew over a much wider area than frankincense, and the kingdom of Qataban was the major producer. They are still found there. The myrrh tree has a central trunk and grows up to about 6 metres in height, with ash-coloured, thorny branches which spread rather like those of a cedar tree. Greenish-white flowers appear in spring, followed by the leaves in late August or early September[10].

The sailors also told Theophrastus how the frankincense and myrrh were collected: 'While the stems looked as if they had been cut with an axe, in the branches the incisions were slighter; also... in some cases the gum was dropping [onto mats], but... in others it remained sticking to the tree... which... they scraped off with iron tools.'

Nowadays frankincense and myrrh trees are cut with a special knife, or *mengeb*, with a blade at each end of a wooden handle, a sharp one for making incisions about 15 cm long, the other (which has a rounded edge) for scraping off the tree the lumps of accumulated gum resin, which take ten days to three weeks to harden.

Theophrastus gives no indication of the season in which the trees were harvested; but according to the Roman Pliny, writing some 300 years later, it was at the time of the dawn rising of the dog-star Sirius, in the hot dog-days of early summer, that the first crop of frankincense was taken. The first incisions were made at the beginning of the hot weather, sometime in April or May, and the gum that oozed out and hardened would be collected about seven to ten days later, when new incisions were made. Collecting and re-cutting would continue until the summer monsoon rains began, usually in July. This, Pliny wrote, used to be the only harvest, but the vastly increased demand that occurred when the Romans joined the incense-users' club had induced the Arabs to introduce a second crop, cutting the bark in winter and harvesting in spring, but it was of inferior quality.

Once the frankincense and myrrh had been harvested, Theophrastus was told, the lumps of gum resin were brought from all the growing areas and collected into 'the temple of the sun' which – unlike the inland collection points – was under armed guard. Each grower put his crop in separate heaps, with a tablet stating the quantity and the price required. When the merchants arrived, they looked at the tablets, chose the heaps that pleased them and took them away, leaving the money on the spot where the incense had been. Next it was the turn of the priests, who took one third of the money – 'for the god' – and left the rest for the grower to collect on his return.

Between September and November, after the end of the summer monsoon, the merchants took the incense to the coast on the first stage of its long journey. At various points along the coast the incense was collected, loaded onto boats and rafts and shipped westwards to the port of Qana, the start of the overland route to the Mediterranean. From there great camel caravans took it to Shabwa, capital of ancient Hadhramaut; then on, coasting in a great loop around the harsh desert of Ramlat as-Sabatayn, putting in at the capitals of the other great kingdoms as though they were ports around an ocean of sand – first Timna, capital of Qataban, then Marib of the Sabaeans, and Qarnaw of the Minaeans.

From the early fourth century BC, well before Alexander the Great, until centuries after his death, the Minaeans appear to have controlled the trade route from their own territory, through Madina, and at least as far as the oasis town of Dedan (now al-

SHABWA, CAPITAL OF THE INCENSE-GROWING KINGDOM OF HADHRAMAUT, WAS
ONE OF THE STAGING POSTS ON THE SOUTHERN PART OF THE INCENSE ROUTE.
HERE, ACCORDING TO THE ROMAN HISTORIAN PLINY, A TEN PER CENT TAX WAS
TAKEN BY THE PRIESTS.

THE BAY OF QANA, WITH THE VOLCANIC OUTCROP OF HUSN AL-GHURAB
BESIDE IT. IN NABATAEAN TIMES SMALL BOATS AND RAFTS BROUGHT THE
HARVESTED GUM RESIN OF THE FRANKINCENSE TREES TO THE GREAT PORT HERE
FROM COLLECTING CENTRES FURTHER EAST ALONG THE COAST; HERE IT BEGAN
THE LONG OVERLAND ROUTE TO THE MEDITERRANEAN.

Khurayba in the Hejaz) where they had a trading colony. To judge from Minaean inscriptions in Wadi Rum, the Jawf oasis, Gaza, Egypt and the Aegean island of Delos, they clearly did not stop in Dedan; and two second-century BC writers, Agatharchides of Cnidus and Artemidorus of Ephesus, both report Minaean traders operating in Palestine.

Eratosthenes of Cyrene, one of the greatest of the ancient Greek scholars, wrote a seminal *Geography* in the third century BC which survives only in excerpts in the works of later writers, in particular that other Greek geographer, Strabo, who wrote in the early first century AD. Eratosthenes was unique in not basing his account exclusively on people who knew only the coasts of Arabia. He discussed the inhabitants, soil and plants between 'the northerly, or desert, part of Arabia' and Eudaimon Arabia, in 'the extreme parts towards the south', and said that the merchants took 70 days to travel between Ma'in and Aela (Aqaba).

While some Minaean traders clearly operated further north, others may well have sold all or part of their stock along the way. Dedan was very near the territory described by both Eratosthenes and Hieronymus as inhabited by the Nabataeans by the fourth century BC. It was from the Minaeans that the Nabataeans must have procured the 'frankincense and myrrh and the most valuable kinds of spices', which in Alexander's day they were already taking on the final stage of their journey to the Mediterranean. It is unclear if the Nabataeans were acting as merchants, or as guarantors of safe passage through their territory and providers of services – water, food, protection – though their active involvement seems likely. They certainly imposed heavy taxes on the goods of others that passed through their lands. What is clear is that when the Minaean kingdom disintegrated in the late second century BC, the Nabataeans took increasing control of the northern parts of the incense route.

Leaving the Hejaz, the camel caravans came into the south of today's Jordan and across long stretches of arid desert. Then they could either descend directly into Wadi Araba, part of the Great Rift Valley, before climbing westwards into the Negev desert; or they could climb onto the eastern plateau that runs north to Petra and Damascus. To reach Gaza, the main port for export to Europe, they had to cross the Negev; but the Negev lay close to people who had a deep interest in the precious aromatic cargoes that the Nabataeans were conducting to the sea – first the Greeks, then the Judaeans, and later the Romans.

To protect their investment, the Nabataeans chose difficult routes across the Negev, through hidden gullies and protected

KHIRBET QASRA, ONE OF THE FORTS ESTABLISHED BY THE NABATAEANS TO PROTECT THEIR TRADE ROUTE THROUGH THE NEGEV DESERT.

wadis, and zigzagging their way up near-vertical cliffs. At strategic points they established forts, each with a cistern, and garrisoned them; and they built caravanserais at places with a permanent water source sufficient to supply the needs of a large caravan. The final stretch was through open terrain which needed more protection, and at Oboda, at the beginning of this last lap, the largest military camp of all was established.

The growth of Rome had ushered in a period of almost obsessive incense burning. Besides its uses in medicine and worship, no Roman funeral was complete without vast quantities of frankincense whose fragrant smoke was thought to put in a good word to the gods for the welfare of the departed in the afterlife. As demand rose, so did the prices. For those involved in the incense trade the profits were considerable, but they were shared between the traders, the tax authorities of the lands through which they travelled, and the producers. According to Pliny, the overland route from south Arabia to the Mediterranean:

is divided into 65 stages with halts for camels. Fixed portions of the frankincense are also given to the priests and the king's secretaries, but beside these the guards and their attendants and the gate-keepers and servants also have their pickings: indeed all along the route they keep paying, at one place for water, at another for fodder, or the charges for lodging at the halts, and the various octrois [tolls]; so that expenses mount up to 688 denarii per camel before the Mediterranean coast is reached; and then again payment is made to the customs officers of our empire.[11]

A BEDOUIN WATERS HIS CAMELS AT A WELL ON THE TRADE ROUTE IN WADI ARABA – ONE OF SEVERAL THAT HAVE BEEN USED CONTINUOUSLY SINCE EARLY NABATAEAN TIMES. THE ANCIENT TRADERS WOULD HAVE HAD TO PAY FOR THE WATER THEY TOOK.

At the time of Augustus a *denarius* weighed 3.89 gm of 98 per cent pure silver; multiply that by 688 and we get 2.676 kg of expenses money that were carried along with the trade goods. It is interesting to compare the modern value of silver with that of Augustus' day: today 2.676 kg of 98 per cent pure silver would sell for around £2580/$4200. Reckoning a fair long-distance camel load at around 180 kg, and subtracting the amount needed for expenses, this leaves just over 177 kg of frankincense to sell at Gaza for an average of 7.35 *denarii* per kg (assuming it at half the retail price in Rome, on Pliny's reckoning). On this basis the trader would receive 1301 *denarii* per camel load, less the 688 for expenses, leaving him a profit of 613 *denarii*, or 2.385 kg of silver – a total of about £2300/$3800 profit on each camel load at today's prices. We do not know how many traders shared this profit by taking different sections of the route; nor do we know how much the producers were paid – though we can assume it would not have seriously dented the traders' profits. Multiply the profit per load by the hundreds of camels in each caravan, and the figures are impressive. We do not know how many caravans plied the route each year, but if the state (as is likely) owned several thousand camels, the Nabataean coffers must have resounded to the cascade of silver.

Some Nabataeans, instead of picking up the trade in mid-route, may have travelled south at an early stage in their trading history in search of the source of these enriching aromatics. We know from Strabo that when the Romans sent an expedition to southern Arabia in 26–25BC they employed a Nabataean as guide. This Syllaeus was clearly not the first Nabataean to reach Marib, the Sabaean capital and home of the most magnificent and renowned water-control system in the ancient world. The dam and temples of Marib must have dazzled the eyes of any of the early Nabataean traders who may have ventured there, for they were so far removed from their own nomadic life-style. And these extraordinary monuments may have crowded some visionary imaginations with schemes to go and do likewise in the territories of northern Arabia that were under their own command.

TWO

INTO A HABITATION OF DRAGONS

Settling in the land of Edom and the
Emergence of the Kingdom

DRAMATIC SANDSTONE CLIFFS RISING FROM A SANDY BASE CHARACTERIZE THE LANDSCAPE OF WADI RUM, PART OF PTOLEMY'S PATRIMONY AFTER THE DIVISION OF ALEXANDER'S EMPIRE.

S OON AFTER ALEXANDER THE Great died in Babylon in 323 BC his unwieldy empire was torn apart in an unseemly power struggle between his generals. When the dust of battle had settled, Seleucus emerged as the ruler of northern Syria and Mesopotamia, while Ptolemy took Egypt, Palestine, Jordan and southern Syria. For the previous ten years the veteran Antigonus the One-Eyed, Alexander's able governor of Phrygia, had controlled much of Asia Minor. Now, facing the rival ambitions of Seleucus and Ptolemy, both considerably his junior, his power base felt constrictingly narrow and he conceived the grand design of reconstituting Alexander's empire under his own rule.

Antigonus moved south with his army and mopped up the whole of Syria, first the area controlled by Seleucus, then that of Ptolemy. This brought him to the northern borders of Edom, the part of Ptolemy's inheritance then dominated by the elusive, desert-wise and very wealthy Nabataeans. They became his next target. Around 312 BC he appointed his friend Athenaeus to attack them, equipping him with 4000 foot-soldiers and 600 horsemen; and he ordered him, once he had defeated the 'barbarians', to take all their herds as booty.[1]

Although Hieronymus of Cardia portrayed the Nabataeans of this time as herders and nomads, they were clearly already in a process of metamorphosis for they had acquired possessions that were not easily transported in a nomadic life. Such immovables needed protection, and for this they must have had at least a general concept of central organization. They had, we are told, a special rock (*petra*), which was virtually impregnable since it had only one path to the top, and there they stored their most valuable possessions. This included a large quantity of

silver — perhaps the Nabataean tribal reserves — and also frankincense, myrrh and other trade goods not currently in transit along the caravan routes. In particular, while the men were away at their regular 'national gathering' — a kind of trade fair — all these precious commodities, together with their old folk, women and children, were left for safe-keeping on the top of this rock.

Athenaeus waited for the time of this trade fair before attacking the rock by night. In the absence of able-bodied men, he captured it easily, killed many of the defenceless people on the summit, took others prisoner and left the wounded to fend for themselves. Loading themselves with as much frankincense and myrrh as they could carry, and 500 talents (13.7 tonnes) of silver, Athenaeus and his soldiers set off in the direction from which they had come as fast as their heavy loads of booty would allow. They aimed to get well away before the Nabataeans learned of the attack and came in pursuit. But it seems the Greeks miscalculated, either as to how soon the Nabataeans would hear what had happened, or as to how fast they could travel, knowing the terrain well and unladen. Horses are far from ideal vehicles in this rocky and arid terrain, and the Greeks' progress must have been slow; they may have been unaware of the superior qualities of camels. The Nabataeans, on the other hand, were not only expert camel riders, they had also developed a camel saddle that was highly efficient for military use.

After about 36 km the Greeks made camp and, being both exhausted and confident that they were safe from pursuers, they slept without keeping proper watch. The 8000-strong force of Nabataeans, having been tipped off by prisoners who had managed to escape, fell upon the Greeks: 'most... they slaughtered where they lay; the rest they slew with their javelins as they awoke and sprang to arms... all the [4000] foot-soldiers were slain, but of the [600] horsemen about fifty escaped, and of these the larger part were wounded'.

At least some of these successful Nabataeans were literate for they wrote a letter of complaint to Antigonus 'in Syrian characters' – Aramaic, the lingua franca of the Middle East – in which they justified their slaughter of the Greeks in terms of self-defence. The two-faced Antigonus the One-Eyed replied soothingly that they had indeed been justified, and that Athenaeus had acted contrary to orders. Wisely the Nabataeans suspended belief and posted watchmen in the hills. After an interval filled with lulling protestations of friendship, Antigonus sent his son Demetrius (who, though young, had already merited the nickname 'Besieger of Cities') with the same infantry force as before, but 4000 horsemen instead of Athenaeus' 600 – they had clearly not perceived the problem with horses in such terrain. Each soldier carried several days' supply of 'food that would not require cooking'.

With the confidence of inexperience, Demetrius seems to have thought that this large force could pass unnoticed. It must have surprised him to find the Nabataeans ready for him. They had, as canny bedouin, scattered their multitudinous flocks in secret areas of their inhospitable terrain, and they had garrisoned the rock. On the first day Demetrius' forces could make no headway against the Nabataeans in their commanding position above them, and at nightfall they withdrew. The next morning, as the Greeks again approached the rock in battle order, one of the 'barbarians' shouted a message:

> King Demetrius, what do you want, or who compels you to make war against us? We live in the desert and in a land that has neither water nor grain nor wine, nor anything that is counted a necessity of life among you... We have chosen a life in the desert, ... causing you no harm at all. We therefore beg both you and your father not to harm us but, after accepting our gifts, to withdraw your army and from now on to regard the Nabataeans as your friends. Even if you want to, you cannot stay here for many days since you lack water and all other necessities.

The hopelessness of his mission must have been sharply brought home to Demetrius – the rock was fully defended and therefore impregnable; and the stinging logic of his lack of water and his diminishing supplies was all too easy to grasp. Demetrius withdrew his army; but with a flash of accustomed arrogance he 'ordered the Arabs to send an embassy about these matters'. The Nabataeans did not make the mistake of sending leaders or fighting men as ambassadors – people who, if taken hostage, might make powerful bargaining chips in the hands of the Greeks. Instead they sent some of their oldest (and possibly wisest) men who repeated and elaborated the arguments that had been outlined in the shouted message. To ease Demetrius' hard decision (he would, after all, have to explain to his father why he had abandoned his task) they also offered gifts of 'the most precious of their products'. By such diplomatic bribery did they persuade him to make terms with them.

Demetrius undoubtedly reported the story differently. A later Greek historian, Plutarch, in his partisan *Life* of Demetrius, maintained that 'by his cool and resolute leadership he so over-awed the barbarians that he captured from them 700 camels and great quantities of booty and returned in safety'. At the time, Demetrius' father was unimpressed and rebuked him for not punishing the Nabataeans – it would only make them more presumptuous, he said, as they would think that they had been spared because of Demetrius' weakness rather than because of his kindness. If that was what the Nabataeans thought, they were probably right.

Throughout the episode the Nabataeans had played their hand with adroit cool-headedness. They had shown implacable military skills when they had to, inflicting a terrible slaughter on Athenaeus' sleeping army; they had answered craft and guile with

IBEX (*CAPRA IBEX-NUBIANA*), INDIGENOUS IN THE SANDSTONE MOUNTAINS OF SOUTHERN JORDAN AND IN THE NEGEV, WOULD OFTEN HAVE BEEN SEEN BY TRADERS EN ROUTE BETWEEN THE NORTHERN ARABIAN PENINSULA AND THE MEDITERRANEAN.

THE PROMINENT ROCK OF
UMM AL-BIYARA LOOMS
OVER THE CITY OF PETRA.
WAS THIS THE 'ROCK THAT
HAS ONLY ONE APPROACH'
WHERE THE NABATAEANS
STORED THEIR PRECIOUS
RESERVES OF FRANKINCENSE,
MYRRH AND SILVER?

their own equal measure; they had kept constant watch for intruders and had armed as soon as they heard that Demetrius and his army were approaching. They had also shown impressive diplomatic skills and at the crucial moment had played their strongest card – their enemy's inability to survive in harsh terrain – to convince the Greeks that they could not win. Finally they negotiated a peaceful settlement, offering rich gifts to sweeten their enemy's bitter humiliation at being outmanoeuvred by 'barbarians'. They had used logic and logistics, and their wealth, with consummate skill. The pragmatism and diplomacy they had displayed – for the first time to the 'civilized' world – were repeated in different ways, and developed, over the following centuries in their relationships with their neighbours.

It is usually assumed that the *petra* of those early Nabataeans, with its one approach, was located in the rocky place that later became their capital city – Petra. A high rock, today known as Umm al-Biyara (mother of cisterns), towers nearly 330 m above the ancient capital, its *genius loci*, with grooved and slanting strata of russet sandstone leaning over the city below. There is only one path that leads to the top, and it is tempting to think that the first known incident of Nabataean history might be set in the heart of Petra. A major problem with this identification, as Dr Fawzi Zayadine has pointed out,[2] is that the account specifies the rock as 300 *stades* (about 54 km) from the Dead Sea, while Petra is more than 100 km from it. Only if we can assume a glaring lack of precision in Hierony-

mus' distances, can Petra have any claim to be the ancient 'rock' of the Nabataeans.

But Umm al-Biyara is not the only rock in the region with a single tortuous path to the top; such rocks are common. About 50 km north of Petra, near the old Edomite capital Bozrah, is a village whose name, Sela, is the ancient Semitic word for 'rock', as *petra* is the Greek. Nearby is a high rock with only one path, and both the approach and the hilltop abound in Nabataean remains – cisterns, houses and sacred niches of the great god Dushara. The rock's early importance is underlined by the discovery,[3] in 1994, of a relief carving halfway up a high cliff, portraying a figure in a long Babylonian kingly robe and pointed cap, a sceptre in his right hand and his left hand raised towards a crescent moon, a winged sun and a seven-pointed star. The cuneiform inscription has not yet been fully deciphered. The close similarity between this figure and one in which the king is named, on a stele found in Harran in southern Turkey, has led scholars to suggest that the Sela relief portrays the Babylonian King Nabonidus who led an expedition into Edom in 552 BC. Perhaps the Nabataeans, as they increasingly occupied Edomite territory, adopted this special rock as a place of refuge and safekeeping. Since it is about 300 *stades* from the Dead Sea, it must have a strong claim to be the place where the Nabataeans entered the world stage of recorded history.

Nobody knows when the Nabataeans first infiltrated the land of Edom – or Seir, as part of this area was often called in ancient times. Seir may have been first mentioned as early as the fourteenth century BC, but it was certainly referred to a century later in some inscriptions of Pharaoh Rameses II. Over the next two centuries, the Pharaohs or their officials from time to time referred to the punishments they inflicted on 'the Shosu tribes' of Edom or Seir, who are depicted as nomadic pastoralists and marauders.

The Old Testament story of the Exodus of the Israelites from Egypt is traditionally dated to around 1270 BC – though it has to be said that some scholars doubt that it happened at all. The biblical account paints a strikingly different picture of the Edomites from that in the Egyptian inscriptions, for it portrays a unified people with a centralized government. We are told that the 'king' of Edom refused Moses' request for the Israelites to pass through his land, and that the Edomites 'marched out with a powerful army' to make compliance more certain. This account – probably written down for the first time in the seventh century BC, about 600 years after the Exodus is deemed to have taken

A SIXTH CENTURY BC RELIEF PORTRAYING THE BABYLONIAN KING NABONIDUS, CARVED HIGH ON A SHEER CLIFF AT SELA. THIS ROCK IS A STRONG CONTENDER TO BE THE PLACE WHERE THE NABATAEANS ENTERED THE WORLD STAGE OF RECORDED HISTORY.

place – was the work of opponents of the Edomites. The Judaean scribes may have wished to minimize the humiliation of their people by inflating the power and organization of the Edomites in those long-distant days. What they describe is very like Edom at the time the Exodus story was being written; it does not at all resemble what we know of this area in the thirteenth century BC.

The total lack of archaeological evidence for settlements in any part of Edom during this period supports the Egyptian view. If there was a more settled section within Edomite society, we know nothing about it, and there is no evidence for anything resembling a unified kingdom with an army. So Edom apparently remained until the early tenth century BC, when – again, only according to the Old Testament – the Edomites may have been on the brink of establishing a unified monarchy. At this point, we are told, King David sent in his Israelite army; 18,000 Edomites were said to have been killed, Edom was garrisoned throughout, and the surviving population enslaved.[4] As if this were not enough, David's general, Joab, 'remained there six months until he had cut off every male in Edom'.[5] Since the Edomite people continued to exist, this was clearly hyperbole.

The Old Testament tells us that Edom remained in subjection to Judah with no central government of its own until, in the mid-ninth century BC, a successful revolt restored the Edomite line of kings to a fragile independence that seems to have lasted about a century. Though Assyrian records mention that Edom paid tribute, it seems likely that Assyria, at this stage in decline, exercised no real authority.

Everything changed in 732 BC when King Tiglath-pileser III extended Assyrian control over Edom, Judah and their neighbours. Within two years his scribes were writing of the kings of Ammon, Moab, Ashkelon, Judah and Gaza, and King Qosmalak of Edom, together presenting costly tribute to the Assyrian king: 'gold, silver, tin, iron, antimony, linen garments with multi-coloured trimmings, garments of local production made of dark purple wool,... and all kinds of precious objects, products either of the sea or the land'.

Despite being a vassal state, providing tribute and occasional military support to the Assyrian kings, and even some

By the end of the seventh century BC Assyrian might was in decline, and in 612 their capital, Nineveh, and their large empire fell to the new power in the Middle East – the second Babylonian Empire. In 587 BC, King Nebuchadnezzar destroyed Jerusalem and took the king and leaders of Judah into captivity to Babylon. There is no independent evidence that the Edomites either supported the Babylonian destruction of Jerusalem or, after the event, grasped the opportunity for a large-scale takeover of the Judaean Negev; but the Judaeans seem to have believed it and never forgave what they regarded as the treachery of their Edomite 'brothers'. In the name of their God, the prophets of Judah and Israel anathematized the Edomites for having 'shed the blood of the children of Israel by the force of the sword in the time of their calamity'; and because they had 'appointed my land into their possession with the joy of all their heart, with

King Tiglath-pileser III of Assyria, soon after his accession in 732 bc, exacted costly tribute from King Qosmalak of Edom, together with the kings of Ammon, Moab, Ashkelon, Judah and Gaza. (Ancient Art and Architecture Collection)

The remains of a seventh century BC Edomite settlement, built on top of the rock of Umm al-Biyara at a time of expansion of the Edomite kingdom. By the following century it was abandoned.

forced labour, the kingdom of Edom appears to have remained largely autonomous. Indeed, the century or so of Assyrian overlordship brought a level of political and economic stability that enabled the Edomites to enjoy the greatest prosperity they had known. They doubtless profited from the passage through their land of major trade routes – one connecting Egypt and Arabia in the south with Syria and Asia Minor in the north, and also the last leg of the journey of the rich caravans bearing incense and spices from Arabia Felix to the Mediterranean. In addition, the Edomites were again mining and smelting copper in Wadi Araba, both for their own use and for trade, and they exploited their fertile pockets of land and abundant springs to develop agriculture and to support their flocks and herds. Prosperity brought an expansion of settlements within Edom itself; and some scholars believe that it was at this period that some Edomites may have begun to settle in unpopulated areas on the fringes of the Negev, apparently without coming into conflict with the people of Judah to whom the territory belonged.

RICH AGRICULTURAL LAND AT THE SOUTHERN END OF THE DEAD SEA, ONE OF THE FERTILE POCKETS EXPLOITED BY THE EDOMITES AT THE NORTH-WEST EDGE OF THEIR TERRITORY. THE PERENNIAL WATERS OF WADI HASA NEARBY HAVE ENABLED THIS AREA TO BE CULTIVATED SINCE EARLIEST TIMES UP TO THE PRESENT.

despiteful minds'.[6] Again speaking on God's behalf, they poured out on the people and the land of Edom vitriolic prophecies of doom:

> For my sword... shall come down on them, and upon the people of my curse, to judgement... And the streams thereof shall be turned into pitch, and the dust thereof into brimstone, and the land thereof shall become burning pitch. It shall not be quenched night nor day; the smoke thereof shall go up for ever: from generation to generation it shall lie waste; none shall pass through it for ever and ever... And thorns shall come up in her palaces, nettles and brambles in the fortresses thereof: and it shall be an habitation of dragons.[7]

Reality, though hard to estimate, may not have been as dramatic as the prophecies suggest. Certainly, by the time of Nabonidus' invasion of Edom in 552 BC, the Edomite kings had disappeared; but the people remained, and it is assumed that they were directly ruled from Babylon until 539 when the Babylonian Empire fell to the Persians. The main interest of these new overlords lay in the trading areas of the Hejaz just

'THE STREAMS THEREOF SHALL BECOME PITCH... AND THE LAND THEREOF SHALL BECOME BURNING PITCH... FROM GENERATION TO GENERATION IT SHALL LIE WASTE'. THIS UNTAMED LANDSCAPE OF THE EASTERN NEGEV, WHICH THE EDOMITES WERE THOUGHT TO HAVE OCCUPIED, LOOKS LIKE A FULFILLMENT OF ISAIAH'S PROPHECY.

south of Edom, and in the rich Mediterranean ports. There is little evidence of their rule in the lands east of the Dead Sea rift, and at most they seem to have exercised only a light control. At some point in the second half of the sixth century BC Edomite settlements were destroyed or abandoned. Throughout Edom, people whose families had for several generations been settled in villages and towns probably pulled up their roots and reverted to a life on the move.

Some Edomites may at this time have settled in the more productive and relatively unoccupied lands west of Wadi Araba, where they were caught up in the Hellenistic world and became known by the Greek form of their name, Idumaeans. Under the Hasmonaean ruler John Hyrcanus the Idumaeans were forced to accept circumcision and adopt Jewish law as the price for remaining autonomous – the result, nearly a century later, was the emergence of an Idumaean, Herod the Great, as king of Judaea, with important consequences for the history of the world and also for the Nabataeans.

Although there is no record of the Nabataeans' first appearance in Edom – the 'habitation of dragons' of the Authorized Version of the Bible – it is known that the trade routes had perennially brought different groups of Arabian merchants taking their cargoes of frankincense, myrrh, spices and gold from Arabia to the Mediterranean. The first groups of Nabataeans who filtered into Edom from the south, working this route, inevitably came into contact with the tribes of Edom who, by the late-sixth century BC, had reverted to a pastoral and nomadic life.

Soon after Nabonidus' incursions many Nabataean groups moved into Edom, wandering throughout the territory with their camels and sheep with no government to challenge them. Several stayed and some no doubt interacted, or even intermarried, with Edomite tribes, for later we find the Edomite god Qos in the Nabataean pantheon. Other Arabian tribes also moved into Edom, but it was the Nabataeans who prospered most. Their pastoral base, their command of desert travel thanks to the use of camels, their abundant wealth from trade, and their acquisition of formidable military skills had made them the dominant group in Edom by the time Antigonus the One-Eyed tried to take over their land and their wealth in the late fourth century BC.

Spices and incense were not the only goods in which the Nabataeans traded. By the time of Antigonus' vicarious attacks they were also lucratively engaged in two other areas, in which

they seemed to have a monopoly. They harvested balsam from the groves 'in a certain valley in this region' (the Jordan Valley near Jericho), for use in medicine; and they also marketed the less fragrant commodity of bitumen which they extracted from the Dead Sea and sold to the Egyptians for use in their embalming process, and for waterproofing boats and pottery. So profitable was the trade in bitumen that the Nabataeans had to vie in the harvesting of it with other peoples who lived around the Dead Sea. According to Hieronymus of Cardia,[8] every year a huge mass of bitumen would appear in the Dead Sea and float on the surface. It would, he wrote, announce its arrival twenty days in advance by a foul smell and an atmosphere that made gold, silver and bronze temporarily lose their colour. When this happened, the Nabataeans made rafts of reeds so that, as soon as the bitumen appeared, they could row out to it. Each reed boat

THE NABATAEANS' USE OF CAMELS AS LONG-DISTANCE CARRIERS AND THEIR CONTROL OF WATER SOURCES HAD GIVEN THEM A UNIQUE COMMAND OF DESERT TRAVEL; AND THE CAMEL SADDLE THEY HAD DEVELOPED WAS HIGHLY EFFICIENT FOR USE IN BATTLE. ALL THESE ADVANTAGES HAD HELPED TO MAKE THE NABATAEANS THE DOMINANT GROUP IN EDOM BY THE LATE FOURTH CENTURY BC.

would have three men — two to row, with oars that were lashed to the boat, and the third man armed with bow and arrows with which to repel competitors. Once they reached the bitumen island, they jumped onto it with axes and chopped out pieces, 'just as if it were soft stone'; then, having loaded it onto the raft, they rowed back to the shore.

Bitumen still appears in the Dead Sea, though very rarely and not in such huge quantities as Hieronymus describes, nor with the malodorous forewarning. The last time a large lump appeared was in 1979 when it was bought by a pharmaceuticals company — for a high price because of the renowned purity of Dead Sea bitumen.

After Demetrius' failure to defeat the Nabataeans, he stayed for a while by the Dead Sea to find out more about the bitumen industry and its profitability. His report to his father on this potential new source of revenue to support their imperial pretensions encouraged Antigonus to send an expedition, led by Hieronymus of Cardia, to collect some bitumen. But this plan also miscarried when the Nabataeans, enraged at yet another Greek incursion, proved as adept at fighting on water as they had been on land: 'for the Arabs, collecting to the number of 6000 and sailing up on their rafts of reeds against those on the boats, killed almost all of them with their arrows'.

Hieronymus clearly survived the hail of arrows to write his history; but 'Antigonus gave up this source of revenue because of the defeat he had suffered and because his mind was engaged with other and weightier matters' — matters that were to lead to his defeat and death at the hands of Seleucus in 301 BC. With Antigonus and his dreams of empire removed, the heirs of Ptolemy and Seleucus had a free hand to fight over control of Syria, Palestine and Jordan. The Nabataeans, who still remained largely nomadic, were little affected by these occasional changes in overlordship between the two superpowers of the day.

Edom was not the only area where the Nabataeans established themselves in the early Hellenistic period. By the fourth century BC they had gained a lucrative foothold all along the incense route from the northern Hejaz, through Edom and into the Judaean Negev towards the Mediterranean coast. They also occupied a stretch of the Red Sea coast and some offshore islands. Diodorus had already, in a sweeping generalization, accused the Nabataeans of being brigands who pillaged their neighbours, but the only direct evidence he produces for their brigandage relates to piracy in the Red Sea. At an unspecified date, some groups of Nabataeans had taken to attacking the richly laden merchant ships of Ptolemaic Egypt; but if they thought they could defy the Ptolemies as successfully as they had defied Antigonus, they were sorely mistaken for 'some time afterward… they were caught on the high seas by some quadriremes and punished as they deserved'.

No reason is given as to why the wealthy Nabataeans should have done so odd a thing as to turn to piracy. An explanation could be that, with the understanding of the nature of monsoons that gradually developed from the late third century BC, the Ptolemaic merchants were beginning to ship Arabian trade goods across the Red Sea directly into Egyptian territory, thus cutting out the overland routes that were the source of the Nabataeans' wealth. The Nabataeans would probably have seen their attacks not as piracy but as legitimate protection of their vital interests under threat from an aggressive competitor.

The second historical mention of the Nabataeans, half a century after Antigonus' aggressions, places them in Auranitis in southern Syria, today's Hauran. This vivid reference — the first to have the authentic ring of a first-hand human encounter — appears in the extensive papyrus archives of Zenon, the right-hand man of Apollonius, minister of finance for Ptolemy II Philadelphos.[9] In 259 BC, while Zenon was on a tour of duty through Judaea, Ammonitis, Auranitis and Galilee, all then under Ptolemaic control, he received a memorandum from Heracleides, one of his chariot drivers. It concerned two fellow-employees, Drimylus and Dionysius, who had been moonlighting into a profitable alternative career selling slave-girls as prostitutes to border guards, temples and local residents in the areas Zenon was visiting. Dionysius had sold one of the girls in Auranitis, and on his return he encountered some Nabataeans who, with 'a shout of protest' at some unspecified misdemeanour, clapped him in shackles and kept him under guard for seven days.

Since this fascinating memorandum makes no suggestion that the Nabataeans were out of place in Auranitis in the mid-third century BC, they were presumably already familiar figures in the area. It is tantalizing not to know the reason for the Nabataeans' protest and reprisals. The most likely options seem to be either that Dionysius had tried to cheat them, or that they were shocked at the price or the nature of the merchandise. In view of the honourable status known to have been accorded women a little later in the Nabataeans' history, and the remarkable equality of their society, it is possible that they were objecting to Dionysius' treatment of women and slaves.

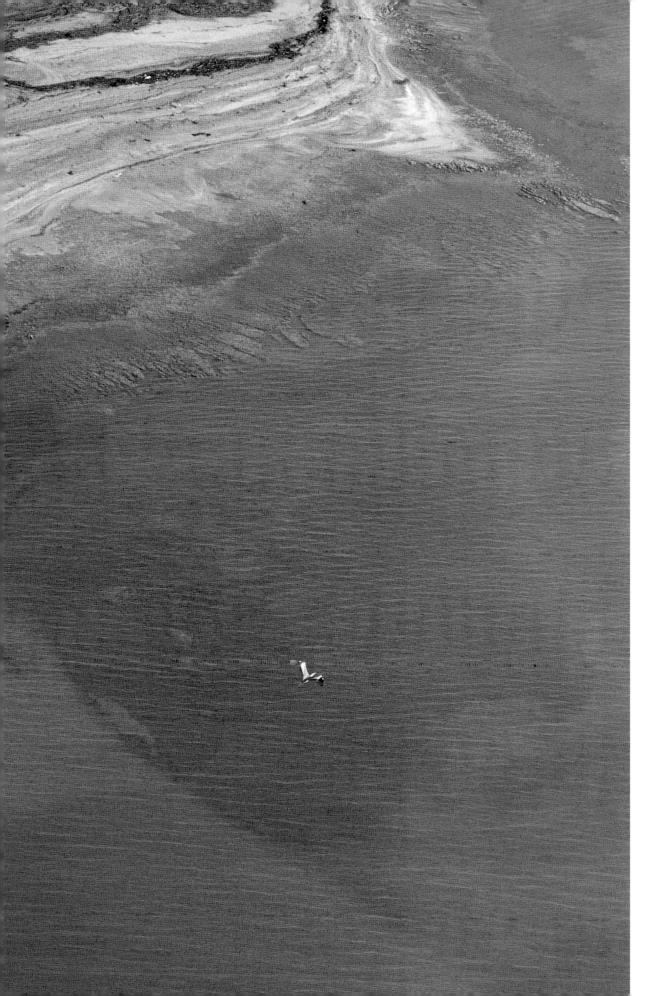

A MIGRATING STORK FLIES OVER THE DEAD SEA, THE LOWEST POINT ON EARTH, FROM WHOSE MINERAL-RICH WATERS THE NABATAEANS HARVESTED BITUMEN, HIGHLY VALUED BY THE EGYPTIANS FOR USE IN THEIR EMBALMING PROCESS. 'ISLANDS' OF BITUMEN STILL APPEAR IN THE DEAD SEA, THOUGH INFREQUENTLY AND IN SMALLER QUANTITIES.

THREE

FRIENDS, FOES AND NEIGHBOURS

Relations with Egypt, Syria and Judaea

SUNSET OVER THE DEAD SEA, WHOSE WATERS DIVIDED THE LANDS CONTROLLED BY THE NABATAEANS ON THE EAST FROM THOSE OF ALEXANDER JANNAEUS AND HIS SUCCESSORS ON THE JUDAEAN THRONE.

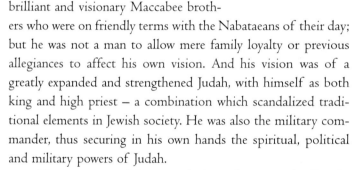HE APPEARANCE OF ARETAS II as king of the Nabataeans coincided with the accession in Judah of the most ambitious and ruthless member of the Hasmonaean family. Alexander Jannaeus (103–76 BC) was a great-nephew of Judas and Jonathan, the brilliant and visionary Maccabee brothers who were on friendly terms with the Nabataeans of their day; but he was not a man to allow mere family loyalty or previous allegiances to affect his own vision. And his vision was of a greatly expanded and strengthened Judah, with himself as both king and high priest – a combination which scandalized traditional elements in Jewish society. He was also the military commander, thus securing in his own hands the spiritual, political and military powers of Judah.

The accession of Jannaeus had not been simple. On the death of his father, John Hyrcanus, his eldest brother Aristobulus had succeeded as high priest and, according to the Roman-Jewish historian Josephus, he was the first Hasmonaean to 'put a diadem on his head'. To eliminate competition Aristobulus had either killed or imprisoned his brothers, and it was from prison that Alexander Jannaeus succeeded when Aristobulus died after only one year. Jannaeus prudently married his brother's formidable widow, Salome Alexandra, for it was she who had engineered his release and succession; and he assassinated another brother who was unwise enough also to cherish aspirations to the throne. Thus he embarked on 27 years of brutal rule, in the course of which he dealt with three gifted and popular Nabataean kings – about whom, unfortunately, considerably less is known than about Jannaeus himself.

It was only by military might that Jannaeus retained his position for he quickly alienated many of his subjects – unsur-

prisingly, his army included a considerable number of foreign mercenaries. He was anathematized by all the religious sects, in particular the Pharisees, who were enraged not only by the high priesthood becoming hereditary outside the traditional high-priestly family, but also by Jannaeus' combining this role with that of king, emulating his short-lived older brother.

Ordinary people also hated Jannaeus, and on one occasion the huge assembly taking part in the ceremonies of the Feast of Tabernacles were so outraged that they pelted him with the citrons they were carrying. To punish them Jannaeus massacred some 6000 Judaeans, and this was followed by civil war from which only the Nabataeans profited as the Judaean king was forced to cede territory to prevent them supporting his opponents. The civil war in turn led to a further appalling act of revenge when Jannaeus ordered 800 of his opponents to be publicly crucified and, while they were still alive on their crosses, that their wives and children be massacred before their eyes; meanwhile, Josephus tells us, 'cup in hand as he reclined amidst his concubines, he enjoyed the spectacle'.[1] This was the man with whom the nascent Nabataean kingdom had to do.

With so much barbarity in Judaea, it is refreshing to turn to the gentler climate of Nabataea, where the gratuitous shedding of blood does not appear to have been commonplace. Brothers are not known to have been murdered or imprisoned to clear the path to the throne for the most aggressive member of the royal family, there is no evidence of civil war, and only once did a senior politician try (unsuccessfully) to usurp the throne. Perhaps by contrast with their neighbours, the Nabataeans have acquired a reputation as a peace-loving people. While this is not entirely misplaced, the theory should not be stretched to unreasonable limits — the Nabataeans were keen to avoid war if diplomacy and gifts could maintain peace, but they had already shown themselves unwilling to bow to outside force, able to defend themselves stoutly and ready to attack if their vital commercial interests were threatened.

The new Nabataean king, Aretas II, remains a somewhat shadowy figure. Our main source of information is Josephus (AD 7–100), who tended to see history from a Judaeo-Roman point of view, and external characters enter his narrative as they affect the story of Judaea[2] and the Roman Empire. It is only later, from the time of Aretas II's grandson, Aretas III, that the Nabataeans begin to come into sharper focus, for by then they were playing an increasingly central role in the story of the ancient Middle East.

Aretas II was described by Josephus as 'a person then very illustrious', and part of his renown may have arisen from his practice, referred to by a later Roman writer,[3] of making armed raids into the territories of the two declining superpowers, Seleucid Syria and Ptolemaic Egypt. He may also have gained renown from minting his own coins — a bold assertion of Nabataean independence, both economic and political, and further evidence of the increasing ineffectiveness of the Seleucids and Ptolemies. Aretas' zest for action also ran in other directions, for he is credited by the same Roman source with having fathered 700 sons from what must have been an impressive clutch of concubines.

So far the Nabataeans had remained at peace with the Hasmonaean state despite the annexation by Alexander Jannaeus' father, John Hyrcanus, of Idumaea and parts of Moab, thus posing a threat to Nabataean trade routes both to the Mediterranean and to Damascus. Now two active expansionists, Jannaeus and Aretas II, faced each other across a border that neither saw as fixed, not least because it included a number of semi-independent

SPRINGTIME IN GALAADITIS (GILEAD OF THE BIBLE), OVERLOOKING THE MODERN RESERVOIR IN WADI ZARQA, ONE OF THE PERENNIAL STREAMS ON THE EAST OF THE RIFT VALLEY. BOTH THE NABATAEANS AND JUDAEANS SOUGHT TO CONTROL MOAB AND GALAADITIS BECAUSE OF THEIR WATER SOURCES.

petty kingdoms and cities which both rulers sought to influence. The inevitable collision came at Gaza. Around 100 BC the city was besieged by Jannaeus on the grounds that the inhabitants had favoured the Ptolemies in their recent battles with the Judaeans. As the siege dragged on, the Gazans appealed to Aretas, with whom they were on good terms – Gaza was, after all, the terminus of the incense route, and the siege must have caused serious problems for the Nabataean trading economy. But Aretas' promised help came too late. The commander of the Gazan army was murdered by his own brother out of jealousy for his popularity, and the city was delivered to Jannaeus who, with his customary lack of concern for human life, put the inhabitants to the sword.

With their main trading outlet to the sea now in Judaean hands, the Nabataeans were faced with a new, more complex and considerably less friendly relationship with their Hasmonaean neighbours. The burden of this fell mainly on Obodas I, one of Aretas II's multitude of sons, who appears to have succeeded his father around 96 BC. In the 11 or so years of his energetic reign, Obodas I changed the map of the Middle East in favour of the Nabataean kingdom. His success can to a great extent be ascribed to his practice of creative interference in the affairs of his neighbours, in particular the Judaeans, using their internal divisions for his own advantage. This was nothing new – the Hasmonaeans had done it for decades, first to win benefits from rival Seleucid kings, and later with the Ptolemies – but it was the first time that it appeared as an underlying principle in Nabataean foreign policy.

When Alexander Jannaeus followed up his father's successes in northern Moab by conquering the rest of the territory, and then Galaaditis, Obodas felt called upon to respond. Though these lands were not under direct Nabataean control, they were apparently within their sphere of influence, and the trade and communications routes to Damascus that appear to have run through them were an economic lifeline. To have them under aggressive Judaean rule threatened not only the Nabataeans but the Damascenes as well. With the help of the Seleucid king, Demetrius III, the Nabataeans fought to wrest control of these vital areas from the Judaeans. Around 93 BC Obodas ambushed Jannaeus and his forces in hilly country in the north of the Nabataean kingdom; using the large numbers of Nabataean camels in the manner of a bulldozer, he pushed the Judaeans into a deep valley from which Jannaeus was lucky to escape alive. With civil war raging in Judaea, Obodas was now

able to exploit the deep divisions among Jannaeus' subjects to his own advantage – so successfully that Jannaeus ceded Moab and Galaaditis to him in order to dissuade the Nabataeans from continuing their support to his opponents.

The acquisition of these two large and rich areas greatly increased the strength of the Nabataean kingdom – and the anxiety of Antiochus XII Dionysus, the new Seleucid king of Syria, who felt threatened by this rising power so close to his borders. In 88–87 BC Antiochus led two campaigns against the Nabataeans which, after some desperate fighting, the Syrians seemed set to win. But Antiochus was killed in action and his demoralized army fled to Cana on the other side of the Jordan

THE HILL COUNTRY IN THE NORTH OF THE NABATAEAN KINGDOM IS FULL OF STEEP-SIDED WADIS. IN ONE LIKE THIS OBODAS I AMBUSHED ALEXANDER JANNAEUS AND HIS ARMY AND THE JUDAEAN KING WAS LUCKY TO ESCAPE WITH HIS LIFE.

PART OF THE RUINS OF OBODA IN THE NEGEV, NAMED AFTER THE DEIFIED OBODAS I, WHO WAS BURIED HERE. OBODA WAS A MILITARY AND RELIGIOUS CENTRE ON THE TRADE ROUTE LONG BEFORE IT BECAME A PLACE OF SETTLED RESIDENCE.

river, where most of them died of starvation. Obodas does not seem to have long survived his victory over the Syrians and may, indeed, have died as a result of wounds sustained in the fighting. He was buried in part of the Negev that was under direct Nabataean rule, at a place that was renamed in his honour – Oboda (today's Avdat). His tomb has never been found.

Obodas' renown following his victories over the Judaeans and the Seleucids amounted to worship, and his people deified him soon after his death – the only Nabataean king for whom we have direct evidence of his inclusion among the gods. A number of rock-cut inscriptions from different periods and different parts of the kingdom refer to 'Obodas the god', or 'Zeus Obodas', indicating that his cult continued even after the Nabataean kingdom had come to an end. One fascinating inscription, possibly dating to around AD 100 and found near the Zin ravine, just north of Oboda, records the setting-up by Garm'allahi, son of Taim'allahi, of a statue dedicated to 'Obodas the god'. Most of it is in the Aramaic language adopted by the

THE KHAZNEH (TREASURY), SITUATED AT THE ENTRANCE TO THE NABATAEAN
CAPITAL, PETRA, IS THOUGHT BY SOME SCHOLARS TO HAVE BEEN
COMMISSIONED BY ARETAS III IN MEMORY OF HIS FATHER, THE GOD-KING
OBODAS I.

could be caught or brought. Numerous cisterns were dug to
catch run-off water during the seasonal rains, and 27 km of covered aqueducts were built into the ground to channel water from
the nearest springs in the escarpment of the Shara mountains.
This regular water supply may have encouraged local bedouin to
come here for trade, and to settle for a while each year to grow
crops, which helped to provision the trading caravans.

It was Aretas III who reaped the benefit of his father's victory over the Seleucids. Soon after his accession, in 85 BC, the
aggressive Ituraeans of the Anti-Lebanon mountains tried to
exploit the power vacuum in Syria by threatening Damascus, and
the Damascenes at once asked Aretas to take over the government. The Nabataean king was only too happy to oblige and
moved in his troops, whereupon the Ituraeans took the hint and
withdrew. Aretas' governor ruled Damascus in his name for
about 15 years. To demonstrate that he was the heir of the Greek
Seleucids, this Arab monarch minted coins in Damascus in the
same Greek style as those of the Seleucids, and with the inscription in the Greek language instead of the Nabataean form of
Aramaic of his own people. This was a temporary and localized
act of cultural vainglory; all later coins minted by his successors
in Petra and elsewhere used the Nabataean script. To make his
Hellenizing pretensions yet clearer, Aretas adopted the epithet
'Philhellene' (lover of Greek culture). The issuing of Nabataean
coins continued in Damascus until 71 BC when King Tigranes of
Armenia captured the city.

In the meantime, Aretas III had not rested on his
Damascene laurels. So far the Nabataeans had not invaded the
Judaean heartland, but in 82 BC Aretas decided to do so and
defeated Jannaeus at the town of Adida, a little to the east of
Lydda. No reason is given for what appears to have been an act
of gratuitous aggression, but it is likely that Jannaeus still held
the Mediterranean ports closest to the Negev, and that this was
adversely affecting Nabataean trade. Aretas may have seen invasion as the only way to force the Judaean ruler to relinquish control of the ports, or at least to reopen them to Nabataean trade.
This was doubtless part of the 'certain conditions agreed on'
after Jannaeus' defeat at Adida, following which Aretas agreed to
withdraw with his army to the east of the Jordan.

Jannaeus was not inclined to leave matters as they now
stood. The next year, feeling stronger again, he marched into the
north of the Nabataean kingdom and, in a three-year campaign,
captured several towns; he also regained control of the
Mediterranean ports of Gaza, Raphia and Rhinocolura. On his
return to Jerusalem after such successes, Jannaeus was greeted
with more enthusiasm than at any other time during his reign.
Although his health was broken by hard drinking and quartan
fever, the ageing Jannaeus threw himself into further strenuous
activities and campaigns which only underlined his increasing
lack of judgement and renewed his unpopularity.

When Jannaeus died in 76 BC he designated his wife,
Salome Alexandra, heir to the Judaean throne. Realizing that his
brutal attempts to reduce the power of the Pharisees had only
succeeded in plunging the country into debilitating civil war,
Jannaeus had advised Alexandra to placate them and give them a
share in the government; it would, he had said, not only secure
her position as ruler, but also ensure that he himself was given a
'glorious funeral'. This Alexandra did. Debarred as a woman
from holding the high-priesthood, she contented herself with
being queen. She appointed her elder son Hyrcanus as high
priest because, by contrast with her activist younger son,
Aristobulus, 'he cared not to meddle in politics, and permitted
the Pharisees to do everything'.

The new situation in Judaea gave Aretas III another chance
for creative interference in his neighbour's affairs, with a view to
redressing his losses of the last few years. Many Jews hated the
Pharisees, resented their new position of authority, and were
ready to seek a foreign alliance so as to force Alexandra to turn
against them, and these dissenters were welcomed at the
Nabataean court. But in 71 BC, before Aretas could profit from
his new allies, the Armenian king had advanced into Syria with
such overwhelming force (Josephus improbably says he had
500,000 soldiers!) that Aretas was obliged to cede Damascus to
him. Even after Tigranes abruptly abandoned Damascus in 69
BC, because the Romans were attacking his homeland, the
Nabataeans made no attempt to regain control there – a surprising omission, given Aretas' evident enthusiasm for the role of
heir to the Seleucids. It created a new power vacuum that the rising super-power, Rome, was able to exploit only five years later.

Meanwhile in Judaea there was a new twist to the tale.
Aristobulus, fretting at his brother's impotence and his own mar-
ginalization, had gathered the support of other anti-Pharisee
elements and captured a number of fortresses in key positions

throughout the kingdom. When Alexandra died in 67 BC, leaving Hyrcanus II as king as well as high priest, Aristobulus and his allies at once moved against his brother. They fought it out in a battle near Jericho from which Hyrcanus fled when his army deserted him. He then sought terms with Aristobulus, agreeing to abdicate both the throne and the high-priesthood in his younger brother's favour, and not to interfere with government.

Aristobulus II had reckoned without the ambitions and diplomatic skills of an Idumaean leader called Antipater, a supporter of the gentle Hyrcanus. This descendant of the Edomites had married Cypros, apparently a woman from a distinguished Nabataean family, who had borne him four sons and a daughter. One of these sons was Herod, the future king of Judaea. Antipater persuaded Hyrcanus to allow him to ask his friend Aretas III for asylum for the dispossessed king, and help in restoring him to his throne. If Aretas thought he had been offered a golden opportunity to take creative interference in Judaean affairs to new heights, he appears to have concealed it at first for it took time for Antipater to persuade him. Finally, in 65 BC, on the promise that the cities that Jannaeus had captured in the last years of his life would be returned to him, the Nabataean king agreed. When the campaign began, Antipater sent his half-Nabataean children for safe-keeping to Petra, thus giving the young Herod and his future adversaries a first-hand view of each other.

Aretas probably did not realize that espousal of Hyrcanus' cause would bring him face to face with the might of Rome. This was not apparent at the outset for the Romans were fully occupied elsewhere. The Nabataeans inflicted a resounding defeat on Aristobulus who took refuge in the temple in Jerusalem, to which Aretas then laid siege. It was at this point that the Romans appeared.

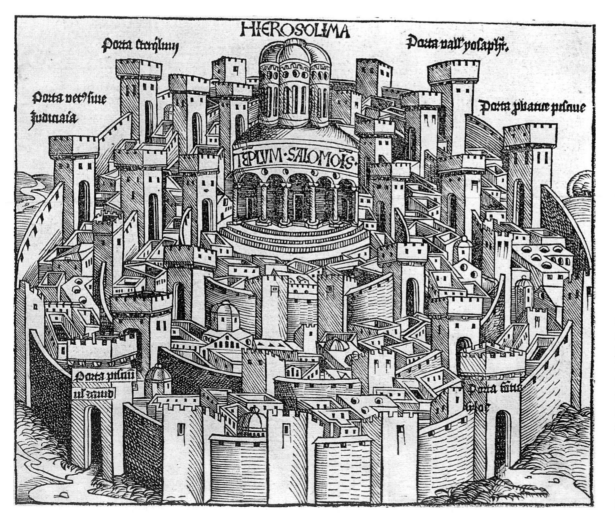

A FIFTEENTH-CENTURY ARTIST'S VIEW OF JERUSALEM AND THE TEMPLE AS THEY MAY HAVE BEEN AT THE TIME THAT ARETAS III HELPED HYRCANUS II TO LAY SIEGE TO THE USURPER ARISTOBULUS C.65 BC. WOODCUT PUBLISHED IN 1493 IN NUREMBURG. (PHOTO: ISRAEL MUSEUM)

As Aretas was beginning his enterprise against Aristobulus, Q. Caecilius Metellus Nepos and L. Lollius, legates appointed by the great Roman general Pompey, moved into Syria while Pompey was finishing his war with Tigranes of Armenia and Mithradates of Pontus. Since Tigranes' departure from Damascus five years earlier, Syria had dissolved into a chaos of warring groups which Metellus and Lollius had little difficulty in subduing in the name of Rome. So successful were they that when their replacement arrived there was little left for him to do. M. Aemilius Scaurus therefore decided to turn his attention southwards – to Jerusalem, where Aristobulus was under siege by Hyrcanus and his Nabataean allies.

Scaurus received delegations from both contenders to the Judaean throne. Both offered bribes, and that of Aristobulus was accepted. It is difficult – especially in view of his later record[6] – not to read venality into Scaurus' actions; but as the bribes were apparently equal in size, he may have had some reasons other than profit, unless he saw Aristobulus' greater wealth and lands as having more potential for the future. It is, in any case, surprising, given their earlier history, that the rich Nabataeans had not inflated Hyrcanus' bribe in order to buy peace on their terms. The shrewd Scaurus, seeing Aristobulus holed up in the temple and besieged by a foreign force, must have realized that if he favoured the older brother, Hyrcanus' Nabataean allies would have a powerful hold in Judaea and thus, despite their reputation for being 'unwarlike', they would pose a threat to budding Roman aspirations in the region. He may have argued that it was wisest to accept the less valid claim of Aristobulus and despatch the Nabataeans as best he could. They could be dealt with separately later.

Pocketing Aristobulus' bribe, Scaurus ordered Aretas to raise the siege and return home; if not, the Romans would invade Nabataea. This chastening prospect persuaded Aretas not to risk his kingdom for the sake of Hyrcanus. He withdrew to Philadelphia (today's Amman), which seems to have remained in Nabataean hands. Supposing the matter was now closed, the enriched Scaurus returned to Damascus. But Aristobulus was loath to leave matters in a way that gave himself no credit; he assembled an army to pursue the Nabataeans and inflicted a shattering defeat on them at a place called Papyron, killing about 6000 (if Josephus is to be believed). Interference had cost Aretas dear and he doubtless returned to Petra to regroup his forces and reassess his position, faced as he now was with a new and energetic superpower, and his enemy ruling in Judaea.

Pompey, the architect of Rome's expansion, arrived in Syria towards the end of 64 BC and immediately annexed the erstwhile Seleucid kingdom, reorganizing it as the new Roman province of Syria. Recalcitrant local leaders were executed or evicted; or, if they agreed to submit, mend their ways and hand over a large sum of money (which helped pay the Roman army), they could remain. Semi-autonomous cities in Moabitis, Ammonitis and Galaaditis, which had been under either Hasmonaean or Nabataean control or had alternated between the two, were freed from both, and their independence was recognized in an area later known as the Decapolis. Ituraea was permitted to remain semi-autonomous under its own prince.

This left Pompey with the considerably more difficult problem of how to handle the two remaining kingdoms – Judaea and Nabataea – which had half a century of mutual hostility behind them. To allow them to remain completely free would be a recipe for continued conflict, while annexation would require enormous force – and the provincial administration already found it difficult to pay its soldiers. To have both kingdoms as friendly clients of Rome probably seemed the best target that current circumstances permitted and, as Judaea was still deeply divided and Nabataea recently defeated, this double reduction may have appeared within the Romans' grasp.

At this point both Aristobulus and Hyrcanus, realizing that Scaurus did not have the last word, reiterated their petitions before Pompey himself, while at the same time the Pharisees urged him to get rid of the Hasmonaean rulers once and for all. In such a riven society every option must have seemed flawed, and Pompey decided to defer a decision until after he had resolved Rome's relationship with the Nabataeans. He therefore 'ordered [Hyrcanus and Aristobulus] to be quiet' and set off southwards with his army. Whether this was for an invasion, or as a show of force to up the ante in Rome's favour in any negotiations, remains open to conjecture. And if it was for a show of force, was the underlying intention to strip the Nabataeans of some of their fabled assets?

We shall never know, for Aristobulus took the opportunity of Pompey's back being turned to raise a revolt in an attempt to secure his position in Judaea. Outraged, Pompey returned at once, abandoning his Nabataean expedition, and took possession of Jerusalem. Though he gave his support to Hyrcanus, thus undoing Scaurus' dubious work of the previous year, the title of king was excised from Judaea – the mild Hyrcanus was appointed high priest and 'ethnarch', or national ruler, but with-

A COIN STRUCK IN HONOUR OF THE ROMAN GENERAL POMPEY THE GREAT,
ARCHITECT OF ROME'S EXPANSION IN THE EAST. HIS ANNEXATION OF SYRIA IN
64 BC BROUGHT THE NABATAEANS FACE TO FACE WITH THE NEW SUPERPOWER
OF THE ANCIENT WORLD. (ANCIENT ART AND ARCHITECTURE COLLECTION)

out royal powers. When Pompey left the area early in 62 BC, to
assert Roman control of Pontus on the death of King
Mithradates, the real power in Judaea was in the hands of his
Jerusalem legate, Piso. Nabataea was the only state to remain
both a kingdom and independent.

Pompey never returned to the Middle East, presumably
convinced that both the new province of Syria and the client eth-
narchy of Judaea were under control, and that the Nabataeans,
with their ally restored to power in Judaea, were unlikely to cause
trouble. On his return to Rome, he was given the unprecedented
honour of a third triumph, in which the dispossessed
Aristobulus was paraded together with captives from Armenia,
Pontus and elsewhere. Pompey's first triumph had celebrated his
victories in Africa; the second, those in Europe; with his new and
yet more glorious triumphs in Asia, Plutarch declared that the
great general had 'led the whole world captive'. The placards carried at the front of the processions named the countries over
which he had triumphed; whether vaingloriously, or as a declaration of future intentions, these included 'Arabia' – Nabataea.
The Roman people were entranced with this exotic and wealthy

new territory on the edges of their latest expansion. The
Nabataean kingdom was on Rome's shopping list.

Pompey had left Syria in the venal hands of Scaurus, with
two Roman legions to support him. He was in a curious position – Pompey had reversed Scaurus' decision by reinstating the
brother he had not supported, and Hyrcanus was an ally of the
Nabataeans with whom Pompey had never reached a settlement.
Whether out of resentment, or a desire for a memorable victory
of his own, or for personal profit – or all three – Scaurus
decided to attack the Nabataean kingdom. Finding the terrain
that bordered his route difficult to manoeuvre in, he set fire to
the fields. At the same time he ran short of supplies and his
army was soon on the point of starvation. This led to a strange
little double-dealing drama in which Antipater, at the request of
Hyrcanus, supplied the Romans with corn from Judaea and then
went to Aretas III, as Scaurus' ambassador, to persuade the
Nabataean king that if he gave Scaurus 300 talents of silver he
would not set fire to Nabataean territory, and the Roman army
would leave. Aretas obliged, thus setting a tempting precedent
for future Roman governors and generals with aspirations to
improve their personal finances.

No amount of wealth ever seems to have been enough for
Scaurus. He overreached himself on his return to Rome in 58 BC
when, while serving as aedile, he spent more money than he pos-
sessed in a vain bid to raise his popularity. One of his expenses
was to strike some coins to commemorate his campaign against
the Nabataean kingdom. With more imagination than accuracy,
he portrayed Aretas III on his knees beside a camel, offering a
branch in submission to the conquering Roman commander –
himself. By this stage Aretas had been dead for four years, and
his successor for one, and Scaurus presumably felt secure that at
such distance his claims were unlikely to be challenged.

Why Aretas was not outraged with Antipater – and also
with Hyrcanus – remains a mystery. Somehow the old Idumaean
fox seems to have enjoyed the trust of his long-standing friend
and ally, as well as that of Rome's representative in the region.
Possibly the Nabataean army had not recovered from its defeat
at the hands of Aristobulus. Possibly, too, Aretas was old and ill
for he appears to have died soon after, leaving one of those tantalizing gaps in the records concerning the Nabataean kings and
their kingdom.

Aretas III appears to have been succeeded briefly by a second Obodas, but the only evidence for him is a handful of silver coins with his name, and the profile of an ageing king – in

marked contrast to the relatively youthful image of the only other Obodas known to have minted coins some 30 years later. Since Obodas II appears too old to have been the son of Aretas III, he may possibly have been a brother. Elderly as he was, in the less than three years of his reign Obodas II is depicted on his coins with different hairstyles – year 1 shows his hair long; in year 2 it is short; year 3 has it back to long again. What is interesting is why he minted coins at all, the first since Aretas III's issues in Damascus. Obodas II's inscriptions are the first in the Nabataean language (the earliest coins had no inscriptions at all, while those of Aretas III used Greek) and, since there are too few coins to have bought anything or paid anyone, the minting seems to be a political statement of continuing Nabataean independence in the wake of Roman inroads in Syria and Judaea, and their two abandoned attempts on Nabataea itself.

The next king, known to us as Malichus I, is also distinguishable from the hairstyle he affected – on his coins he is portrayed as a young man (even after nearly 30 years of rule) whose carefully styled ringlets hang in a vertical fall. A controlled image of dynamic youth, rather than unvarnished verisimilitude, seems to have been thought desirable, perhaps because most of his coins were issued during a time of war.

Soon after Malichus' accession the Nabataeans had another brush with the Romans for in 55 BC Gabinius, Scaurus' successor as governor of Syria, led a successful expedition against them. No reason is given for the attack (profit is one possibility); and whatever negative effects the Roman victory may have had on Nabataean independence, these were soon nullified by nearly two decades of Roman civil wars. These began between Pompey and Julius Caesar in 49 BC, continued with Cassius and Brutus, Caesar's assassins, against Mark Antony and Caesar's unknown heir, Octavian; and would end when Octavian defeated Antony at the Battle of Actium in 31 BC.

Since support was continually being sought by one side or another (or both), the still independent Malichus was required to play the difficult and dangerous game of spot-the-winner in the hectic permutations of Roman power. At first he was advised by the untiringly devious Antipater, who was still the right-hand man of Hyrcanus II. Unswayed by Pompey's earlier support of Hyrcanus, which would have made him a natural ally, or by Julius Caesar's support of Aristobulus, which would have made him a natural enemy, Antipater shrewdly assessed that Caesar had greater staying power. After Aristobulus' murder by Pompey's men, Antipater succeeded in swinging Caesar's support around to Hyrcanus; and in 47 BC, soon after Pompey's death, he persuaded Malichus to join Nabataean military support with that of Judaea in Caesar's final battle at Alexandria which left Cleopatra as queen of Egypt. This did more immediate good to Antipater than to Malichus, for the Idumaean was appointed procurator of Judaea, in which position, thanks to Hyrcanus II's 'slow and slothful temper', he enjoyed almost royal status. This, and the increasing power of his sons, in particular the dynamic and ruthless Herod, turned many Jews against Antipater. His death by poison in 43 BC, within a year of Caesar's assassination, deprived Malichus of a wise, if wily, adviser in the next hard choice of which Roman to support.

Cassius and Brutus had fled east and were successfully forming an alliance against Octavian and the then more famous Mark Antony. Both Antony and Octavian for the time being remained in Italy, leaving all propaganda opportunities in the east to their opponents. The Nabataeans, along with Hyrcanus II who was now advised by Antipater's son Herod, sided with Cassius and Brutus – a bad move, as it turned out, for they were defeated by Antony and Octavian at Philippi in 42 BC. However, when Antony was put in charge of the settlement of the east, his policy of magnanimity towards those who had chosen the wrong side allowed the Nabataeans and Judaeans to switch loyalties, and to benefit from their belated wisdom. In any case, having summoned Cleopatra for political discussions on the position of Egypt in his new scheme of the world, and then having accompanied her back to Alexandria for further non-political intercourse, Antony now had more pressing things to do than to pursue his erstwhile opponents.

To complicate the picture further, Titus Labienus – son of one of Caesar's generals who had defected to Pompey – had persuaded the Parthians to join Brutus and Cassius. After their defeat at Philippi, Labienus took up the cause of Antigonus, son of the dead Aristobulus, thus reigniting conflicts in both the Hasmonaean and Roman camps, for now Antony and Hyrcanus were lined up against Labienus, Antigonus and the Parthians. Though the Nabataeans were not directly involved in the conflict, it was to have important consequences for them.

In the early spring of 40 BC Labienus and his Parthian allies took Jerusalem. Phasael, Antipater's eldest son, was captured and committed suicide; Hyrcanus II was imprisoned and his ears were cut off. Since the high-priesthood could not be held by anyone who was either deformed or mutilated, Hyrcanus was automatically debarred and Antigonus was installed as king and high priest. Herod managed to escape and made his way to Petra, that well known refuge of Jewish dissidents, to seek help from the Nabataean king. If Malichus might have been prepared to give Herod the protection he asked for, he was certainly in no mood to countenance his demand for money and the return of the cities that Herod's father Antipater had restored to Aretas III 25 years earlier. It is astonishing that he made the demand at all; but chutzpah was always one of Herod's predominant traits. Malichus, compared with both Herod and some of his own predecessors, had a cautious streak. Now, seeing a new turn in the fortunes of the Middle East and a decline in Rome's power, he gave his support to the Parthians, who not only had overrun Judaea and Syria but were masters of much of Asia Minor as well.

Leaving Petra, Herod gave an even greater demonstration of chutzpah by taking the momentous decision to go to Rome to lay his bad-luck story before Antony, Octavian and the Senate. Portraying Antigonus as an enemy of Rome, and himself as their proven friend, Herod succeeded in winning such enthusiastic support that the Senate issued an official decree creating him king of Judaea and giving him Roman military support to evict Antigonus and the Parthians from Jerusalem. This was finally achieved in 37 BC, by which time the Roman general Ventidius Bassus had succeeded in driving the Parthians out of Syria and back to their homeland further east. Ventidius also imposed a large fine on the wealthy Nabataeans, thus in a single swipe punishing them for having once again chosen the wrong side and replenishing Rome's depleted coffers. Malichus' compliance indicates that he had once more fallen into line with Rome.

When Antony arrived in Syria in the autumn of 37 BC to reorganize the region, Cleopatra was at his side, very likely less motivated by love than by the hope of finding ways of increasing her reduced domains and wealth. She petitioned to be given Judaea and Nabataea, but it was one of her few desires that Antony refused to satisfy. Infatuated as he was, not even he was prepared to deal so devastating a blow to rulers of whose loyalty he now seemed assured. Instead he compromised, giving her part of the Phoenician coast, Herod's beloved balsam groves near Jericho, and from the Nabataeans, part of Auranitis and a stretch of coast thought to have been on the Red Sea. Herod and Malichus then had to lease back their erstwhile territories for the exorbitant sum of 200 talents each. Herod, doubtless because he was perceived as the closer friend of Rome, was made guarantor of Malichus' payments — an arrangement designed to increase

the bitter enmity that already existed between them. When, a few years later, Malichus defaulted on his payments, Cleopatra persuaded Antony to order Herod to launch a campaign against the Nabataeans — even at the time it looked suspiciously like an elaborately laid plot for the mutual destruction of the two kingdoms so that the Egyptian queen could annexe both.

It is in this two-year period leading to the war with Herod that Malichus' only known bronze coins were minted. They are dated to years 27 and 28 of his reign – 33 to 31 BC – when even the wealthy Nabataean king needed money to pay his troops. Herod's first sally against the Nabataeans was at Diospolis (Lydda), but his victory there was soon followed by a disastrous defeat at Kanatha (present-day Qanawat) in Auranitis, when the Nabataeans were joined by one of Cleopatra's generals, Athenion, who had quarrelled with Herod. The Judaean king's problems were compounded by a devastating earthquake at home which caused such extensive damage that the country was unable to function for some time. Herod sued for peace with the Nabataeans; but Malichus, confident that he had the Judaeans

HEROD THE GREAT, WHO IN 37 BC PERSUADED ANTONY, OCTAVIAN AND THE ROMAN SENATE TO APPOINT HIM KING OF JUDAEA. THIS EARLY THIRTEENTH CENTURY RELIEF PORTRAYS HIM ORDERING THE MASSACRE OF CHILDREN. (MASSA MARTANA CATHEDRAL, ITALY; BRIDGEMAN ART LIBRARY)

A ROMANTICIZED VIEW OF THE MEETING OF ANTONY AND CLEOPATRA BY THE SEVENTEENTH CENTURY ARTIST SEBASTIEN BOURDON. (LOUVRE; BRIDGEMAN ART LIBRARY)

on the run, put his envoys to death. It is one of the few known acts of gratuitous brutality in the Nabataean kingdom. Malichus followed it up by planning an invasion of Judaea.

Herod reacted swiftly. He moved his army, which had been remarkably unaffected by the earthquake, into Transjordan where they met the Nabataean forces in battle near Philadelphia. This time the Judaeans emerged as the victors, and inflicted a crushing defeat on the Nabataeans; but neither the Judaean victory nor the Nabataean defeat in the end made any difference. In 31 BC, at the same time as Herod's and Malichus' war, Antony had been defeated at Actium by Octavian, and the map of the Roman world was once more about to be redrawn, this time by a single immensely powerful ruler. Within a short time Octavian was to become the Emperor Augustus.

On the face of it, Herod had more to worry about than Malichus from the new ruler. Though both had supported Antony, Malichus had been the less enthusiastic. Indeed, so bitterly did he resent Cleopatra's rapacity (and Antony's complicity) that he sent forces to Suez to burn the ships the Egyptian queen had retrieved after Actium and had pulled out of the water there, intending to haul them overland to the Red Sea. Not surprisingly, Octavian reacted positively to this master-stroke and, had Malichus lived, he might well have been rewarded for his diplomatic arson; but he died in the same year and was succeeded by a king of a very different colour. Following Cleopatra's suicide in 30 BC, Octavian annexed her kingdom and from it created the new Roman province of Egypt.

Herod's tactics were predictably different from those of Malichus – he murdered the octogenarian Hyrcanus II, who had again hoped for asylum in Nabataea but whose letter to Malichus requesting it had been intercepted by one of Herod's men. Herod's public excuse for executing Hyrcanus was that his old patron was guilty of treason; he also knew that Hyrcanus' death would conveniently eliminate his only real rival to the throne. Herod now repeated his previously successful bid for Roman support by going to meet those in power; this time he had only one person to deal with – the alienated Octavian, at that moment in Rhodes. Herod knew that he had to put on the performance of his life. He laid down his diadem as a visual demonstration of submission and, with his customary audacity, claimed that his old loyalty to Antony was an indication of his future loyalty to the new Roman *princeps*. It clearly suited Octavian to accept Herod's protestations at their face value; he confirmed him as king of Judaea and added to his kingdom Samaria, parts of the coast and of the Decapolis, and an area near Jericho.

The stage seemed set for the rise of Judaea and the fall of Nabataea. Nobody could have predicted that over the next three decades exactly the reverse was to happen.

FOUR

DAYS OF GLORY, DAYS OF DUST

From Independence to Roman Annexation

'THERE WAS ONE OBODAS, king of Arabia, an inactive and slothful man in his nature; but Syllaeus managed most of his affairs for him'.[1] Thus Josephus, writing just over a century later, introduced Malichus I's gentle successor on the Nabataean throne and his hyperactive chief minister. The contemporary Greek geographer, Strabo, though less scathing about the Nabataean king, draws a similar picture: 'Obodas, the king, did not care much about public affairs, and particularly military affairs... he put everything in the power of Syllaeus.'[2] And in Strabo's eyes Syllaeus was the epitome of deception and wickedness.

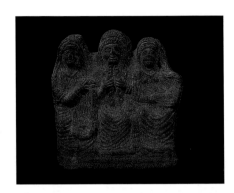

A GROUP OF THREE MUSICIANS — TWO WOMEN ON EITHER SIDE OF A MAN — MADE OF MOULDED EARTHENWARE AND FOUND IN PETRA. THEY ARE SEATED ON A BENCH WITH THEIR FEET ON WHAT LOOK LIKE CUSHIONS; ONE WOMAN PLAYS A LYRE, THE OTHER AN UNIDENTIFIED STRINGED INSTRUMENT, WHILE THE MAN PLAYS A DOUBLE FLUTE. MUSICIANS SUCH AS THESE PERFORMED AT SACRED FEASTS AS DESCRIBED BY STRABO. (AMMAN ARCHAEOLOGICAL MUSEUM)

If Octavian — or Caesar Augustus as he was grandiloquently named by the Roman senate in 27 BC — had turned his attention to Nabataea during the 21 years of Obodas III's reign, the kingdom might have become a Roman province about 130 years earlier than it actually did. Instead, in the early years of his principate, Augustus was captivated with the idea of expanding his rule into the Arabian peninsula; and, he thought, while the expedition was there, it could find the source of the frankincense and myrrh for which the Romans paid so high a price in the market.

Augustus gave the command of the expedition to his governor of the new Roman province of Egypt, Aelius Gallus, a personal friend of Strabo's. Herod, anxious to prove his allegiance to the emperor, sent a force of 500 men while the Nabataeans supplied 1000, including the man who was to act as guide for the expedition — none other than the young and indefatigable chief minister, Syllaeus. With a total force of 11,500, they set out around 26 BC.

It seems extraordinary that the Nabataeans took so active a part in an expedition that they must have perceived as striking to the heart of their commercial interests. It is equally curious that Augustus gave a Nabataean so crucial a role as that of guide. Certainly the Nabataeans — or at least their incense traders — would have known the terrain better than any of the other participants, but they stood to lose the most if the enterprise was a success. The horns of this dilemma must have appeared peculiarly uncomfortable to the Nabataean king — succeed, and you lose much of your trade and the wealth it brings; fail, and you lose the friendship of the most powerful man in the world. But for the ambitious Syllaeus the personal benefits of success would have been considerable — the gratitude, and all that might come with it, of the Roman emperor. There was, of course, a high chance of failure — to take an army, and a largely western army, rather than a peaceful camel caravan into the difficult and arid territory of Arabia Felix was to invite hostility from the people who lived there, who for centuries had guarded their aromatic secrets with the utmost jealousy and who knew the terrain so much better than any outsider.

Augustus' plan, at least for public-relations purposes, was to make allies of the south Arabian peoples in whose lands the incense grew; but should this armed charm offensive fail, the Roman army would have to conquer them. Displaying the breathtaking self-confidence that marked his life, Augustus expected, writes Strabo, 'either to deal with wealthy friends or to master wealthy enemies'. Yet long before reaching the incense kingdoms, the Roman army had been stricken 'by hunger and

THE LANDSCAPE AROUND HEGRA, WHERE, IN c.25 BC, AN AILING ROMAN
ARMY (INCLUDING 1000 NABATAEAN SOLDIERS) WAS LOOKED AFTER BY
ARETAS, THE NABATAEAN GOVERNOR OF THE REGION AND A RELATIVE OF KING
OBODAS III.

fatigue and diseases… the result of the native water and herbs'.
It was not the first time, nor was it to be the last, that western-
ers' constitutions proved unequal to eastern water and food.

After spending several months on the Red Sea coast, 'wait-
ing for the sick to recover', the army moved into the inland areas
of the Hejaz, where the Nabataeans already had a base. Here,
probably in the area of Hegra (today's Meda'in Saleh), which
soon after became an important Nabataean city, the expedition
was received kindly by one Aretas, a relative of King Obodas. He
then sent the revived army on its way south to the once great
trading kingdom of Ma'in, by then in decline. The Romans and
their allies captured the city of Najran without a fight, and
moved further south into the desolate monochrome landscape of

Wadi Jawf, the Minaean heartland. There, after no attempt at
'winning the Arabians over', according to their stated purpose,
they had their first battle with 'the barbarians' (as Strabo called
the Minaeans with withering superiority), 'and about ten thousand of them fell, but only two Romans'. Aelius Gallus established a garrison in a city Strabo called 'Athrula' (today's
Baraqish), which had also fallen without a struggle, and then
proceeded across the fiery eastern plains to Marib, the Sabaean
capital and the greatest city of south Arabia. The Romans must
have wilted at the sight of vast stretches of volcanic lava at the
approaches to Marib – black, razor-sharp and weirdly contorted
from the time of its primeval molten heat – a searing landscape
from their most terrifying nightmares.

Aelius Gallus laid siege to Marib for six days, 'but for want
of water desisted'. It is extraordinary that water was a problem
at Marib of all places, for its famous dam, already at least five
centuries old, lay only a short distance up a fertile valley on the
other side of the city. The Romans seem to have been unaware
of its existence, and the Sabaeans clearly had ways of keeping

THE 'OLD CITY' OF MARIB. BENEATH ITS DESERTED BUILDINGS LIE THE
UNEXCAVATED REMAINS OF THE ANCIENT CAPITAL OF THE SABAEAN KINGDOM,
WHICH THE ROMAN ARMY BESIEGED FOR SIX DAYS. DESPITE BEING NEAR THE
GREAT MARIB DAM, THE ROMANS HAD TO CALL OFF THE SIEGE BECAUSE OF
LACK OF WATER.

them and the water apart. It was the final straw. The expedition
packed up and began the long march home. It took 60 days to
reach the northern Red Sea coast compared with the six months
it had taken them on their way out. This convinced Strabo that
his friend Aelius Gallus had been treacherously misled by the
guide Syllaeus. Fortunately for Syllaeus, Augustus does not seem
to have shared this view. On the contrary, throughout his life the
emperor appears to have regarded the expedition as a success —
his army had penetrated deep into the Arabian peninsula, with
all its supposed wealth from aromatics, they had defeated Arab
armies and captured Arab cities. Not even Augustus' hero
Alexander had achieved this.[3] The fact that the Romans had not
reached the areas where incense was grown was conveniently
overlooked. As for the ambitious Syllaeus, he returned home to
Petra to take up his life where it had left off.

The Petra of Obodas III has been brought vividly to life by
Strabo, whose friend, a philosopher called Athenodorus, had
spent some time there. What he described was a cosmopolitan
city where, apart from the Nabataean population, 'many Romans
and many other foreigners' were living. One thing that particularly impressed Athenodorus was the fact that the Nabataeans
did not indulge in litigation — it was only the foreigners who
raised legal cases, both against other foreigners and also against
some of the Nabataeans. 'The natives', he reported, 'in every way
kept peace with one another', and in his opinion this arose from
the fact that the city was 'exceedingly well governed' by the king
who had 'as Administrator [chief minister] one of his companions, who is called "brother"'. The term did not imply a blood
relationship, but had been borrowed from the courts of the
Hellenistic kings who used it to refer to important counsellors.
For Obodas III this 'brother' was Syllaeus.[4]

These 'sensible people', as Strabo called the Nabataeans,
now lived a life far removed from that described by Hieronymus
of Cardia some 300 years earlier. No longer were they con-
strained by the ascetic principles necessary for a nomadic life —
now, in the security of their capital city, they lived in costly
stone-built houses; and they had become 'so much inclined to
acquire possessions that they publicly fine anyone who has
diminished his possessions and also confer honours on anyone
who has increased them'. While this may appear to refer approv-
ingly to personal materialism, it seems more likely that it was
tribal property that was being so fiercely protected. The
Nabataeans had also become farmers, growing fruits and raising
white-fleeced sheep, large cattle and camels, but no horses. Their
dress was simple, held by a girdle at the hips, and they wore slip-
pers on their feet. Only the king might wear purple.

For all their new materialism, Strabo tells us that slaves, so
common in the Roman world, were noticeably few among the
Nabataeans. This is particularly impressive in view of the volume of architectural projects that were initiated at this period —
both construction of buildings and carving of monumental
tomb façades in the mountains that surround Petra. The large
workforce required for these projects evidently consisted mainly

PETRA, THE CAPITAL OF THE NABATAEAN KINGS, BEGAN ITS MAJOR PERIOD OF
GROWTH IN THE REIGN OF OBODAS III. HERE, ACCORDING TO STRABO, 'THE
NATIVES IN EVERY WAY KEPT PEACE WITH ONE ANOTHER'.

A STONEMASON AT WORK
RESTORING ONE OF PETRA'S
MONUMENTS, USING TOOLS
VERY SIMILAR TO THOSE USED
BY THE NABATAEANS 2000
YEARS EARLIER.

of Nabataean citizens – with the onset of peace, perhaps soldiers had turned their swords into chisels.

The absence of slaves would also have required each person (or his relatives) to perform the host of tasks needful for daily life, and also for their ritual banquets. From Strabo's account it appears these banquets were celebrated in some style, the meal being shared in groups of 13 people who were entertained by two girl singers. Another complete change in attitude from the Nabataeans' nomadic days is seen in his description of the king's drinking feasts, which were held 'in magnificent style, but no one drinks more than 11 cupfuls, each time using a different golden cup.' Since the Nabataeans are known to have produced wine, these eleven cupfuls were presumably not alcohol-free. In this remarkably equal society, even the king was 'so democratic that, in addition to serving himself, he sometimes even serves the rest himself in his turn'. Not only that: he had to give 'an account of his kingship in the popular assembly', a practice that would have found little sympathy or understanding with Obodas III's autocratic contemporaries, Herod the Great and the Emperor Augustus. Perhaps it was the source of his perceived ineffectiveness.

In the reign of Obodas III the profile of the queen appears for the first time on the coins together with that of the king. Though no name is given for her, the fact that she appears at all is an indication of the rising status in Nabataean society of the queen in particular, and probably of women in general. She is portrayed behind the king, so that most of her head, including her hairstyle, is obscured; but Obodas has a fillet tied around the top of his head, from which his hair descends here in tight ringlets, there in pageboy curls. On his early coins he appears as a young man but, unlike his predecessor Malichus I who maintained an image of youth to the end, later in his reign Obodas III allowed himself to be represented with the heavier features of middle age. This acceptance of reality is touchingly in keeping with a king who, against the trend in the contemporary world outside Nabataea, gave his wife an official position on his coins, served others and was prepared to answer for his actions to the people he ruled. But none of these excellent qualities has diminished Obodas' reputation for ineffectiveness, firmly established by the Jewish Josephus and the Roman-Greek Strabo who found nothing to admire in such practices.

On his return from the Arabian expedition, Syllaeus clearly had better things to do than to participate in the gentle lifestyle of Petra. Preferring the sword to the chisel, he set out energetically in pursuit of what he fully intended to be a brilliant career, demonstrating his value as the 'brother' of the democratic Obodas III. He was, according to Josephus, young, shrewd and handsome and these qualities brought him to the notice, while on a visit to Herod in Jerusalem, of the Judaean king's headstrong sister Salome who was, of course, half-Nabataean like her brother. This restless twice-widowed woman – both of whose previous husbands had been executed because of their ambition – was looking for a change of direction; in a short time she and Syllaeus (who in temperament appear to have had much in common) were embroiled in a passionate affair that was the scandal of Jerusalem. Spies reported to Herod 'that by the signals which came from their heads and their eyes, they both were evidently in love'. For Syllaeus, who seems to have overlooked the fate of Salome's two dead husbands, the possibility of a dynastic marriage to the sister of the Judaean king, who was on good terms with the Roman emperor, must have seemed a gift from his gods.

When Syllaeus went to Herod to discuss the marriage he found him unenthusiastic. In an attempt to win favour, he pointed out that he was already the power behind the Nabataean throne, and dropped some unsubtle hints that his position might be even greater in the future – apparently unaware of Herod's long record of resistance to anyone who pursued a high-flying programme of his own. Herod's stipulation that Syllaeus must first convert to Judaism before he could marry Salome rapidly cooled the Nabataean's ardour for he knew that if he did so he would be stoned by his own people. The disappointed Salome was forced to marry the nearest available nonentity, one of Herod's Idumaean courtiers called Alexas, whose lack of ambition doubtless made him acceptable to his brother-in-law.

At the same time as these romantic overtures, Syllaeus had been working against the interests of his would-be brother-in-law, and after the rejection of his suit he doubtless brought greater enthusiasm to these subversive efforts. The original grievance went back to Antony's gift of parts of Auranitis, Trachonitis and Batanaea to Cleopatra. After Actium Augustus had returned these territories, which adjoined Nabataea, to the son of the local ruler from whom they had been taken. This Zenodorus promptly sold or leased his land in Auranitis to the Nabataeans for the bargain sum of 50 talents. The Nabataean king, either from idleness or a sense of independence, had not confirmed his title with Augustus, so when the emperor decided to give the territory to Herod, the Nabataeans were left with neither the land nor the money. Herod was also, at various times, were adorned using new ideas in both carved and painted decoration, executed with great artistry. They developed exquisite pottery of eggshell thinness, painted with delicate monochrome designs. Petra was not the only place where such transformation took place — both the new Nabataean outpost at Hegra (see pages 153–164) in the north-west of the Arabian peninsula, and Bostra, the main city of Auranitis in southern Syria, grew not only in size and in the glory of their new monuments, but also as centres of Nabataean administration. Even the old staging posts along the trade routes through the Negev (especially Oboda, Elusa and Nessana), although not residential, increased in importance as military bases and centres of worship.

It was not only in the Middle East that the Nabataeans had bases which they now expanded and beautified. At Alexandria and Rhodes, at Puteoli on the west coast of Italy near Naples, and elsewhere along the sea routes to Europe, Nabataean merchants had long since established trading bases and temples. Here, so far from home, they could ease their souls in the presence of their own familiar deities. An inscription found at Puteoli records the restoration of 'the former sanctuaries... made in the 8th year [51 BC] of Malichus, king of the Nabataeans'. The renewed sanctuary was dedicated 'for the life of Aretas, king of the Nabataeans, and of Huldu his wife, queen of the Nabataeans, and of their children, in the month Ab [August], the 14th year [AD 5] of his reign'. Six years later two Nabataeans in Puteoli, presumably merchants, put up another inscription to commemorate an answered prayer, and the offerings — probably votive figurines made of precious metal — which they had dedicated in thanksgiving to their great god: 'These are two camels offered by Zaidu, son of Taimu, and Adelze, son of Haniu, to the god Dushara who heard us. In the 20th year of the reign of Aretas, king of the Nabataeans, who loves his people.'

Even at the time these inscriptions were carved, the overland trade in incense, spices, gold and other precious commodities from southern Arabia and the east was gradually being diverted to sea routes that took the merchandise by ship across the Red Sea directly into the Roman province of Egypt. Soon the trend went a stage further, with goods being brought from India by European merchants. This revolution was caused unwittingly by one man.

Around AD 20 Hippalus, a Greek merchant and seaman, noted that from May to October the wind in the Indian Ocean blew steadily from the south-west, while from November to March it blew from the north-east. One summer, following a hunch, he sailed with the south-west wind as far as the Ras Fartak headland on the south Arabian coast; then, instead of hugging the coast as other seamen did, he daringly set off into the open sea. He reached India near the mouth of the Indus, and returned equally successfully in winter with the north-east wind. Hippalus achieved fame as the first European to identify and harness the working of the monsoons; but his discovery spelt the end of the golden centuries of trade for the south Arabians, and for the Nabataeans. From then on the Romans had less and less need to depend on the costly overland route to bring precious incense and spices into Roman territory.

It took several decades for the full effects of Hippalus' revolution to be felt — and, indeed, the land routes never completely dried up during the period of the Nabataean kingdom. Meanwhile, the Nabataeans' increasingly sedentary lifestyle had necessitated an increase in agricultural production, which in turn had necessitated an increase in their means of channelling and storing water. They became water engineers of genius, creating sophisticated irrigation systems in every part of the Nabataean domains — around Petra, and in the Hejaz, the Negev and Auranitis. This capacity to adapt their skills to meet the new needs that confronted them enabled the Nabataeans to survive the gradual decline in their overland trade. From their early near-exclusive dependence on trade, the kingdom was already developing a highly successful economy based largely on agriculture.

Into this picture of cultural and bucolic splendour human relations once again introduced a discordant pattern. In AD 27 one of Herod's sons, Herod Antipas, tetrarch of Galilee and Peraea, paid a visit to the Emperor Tiberius in Rome. While there, Antipas fell passionately in love with his niece Herodias, who was married to one of his half-brothers. To marry her would outrage Jewish religious opinion — not because she was his niece, to whom marriage would have been allowed, but because the law forbade a man to marry his brother's wife while his brother was still alive. Despite this Antipas proceeded to divorce his wife, the Nabataean princess to whom he had been married for many years, which outraged her father, Aretas; and, disre-

HEROD'S HILLTOP PALACE-FORTRESS AT MACHAERUS, JUST EAST OF THE DEAD SEA, TO WHICH ARETAS IV'S DAUGHTER ESCAPED WHEN SHE LEARNED THAT HER HUSBAND, HEROD'S SON HEROD ANTIPAS, PLANNED TO DIVORCE HER. IT WAS HERE, TOO, THAT JOHN THE BAPTIST WAS IMPRISONED AND EXECUTED BECAUSE OF HIS CONDEMNATION OF ANTIPAS' DIVORCE AND REMARRIAGE TO HERODIAS.

moted as a kind of 'life and deliverance', though the Nabataeans' love of liberty would have made it a hard notion to sell. But they must surely have felt increasingly isolated – Judaea to the west, Egypt to the south and Syria to the north had long since been mopped up in Rome's territorial expansion. In the first decade of Rabbel's reign, several local kingdoms and principalities were absorbed into the province of Syria; by AD 93 Herod Agrippa II had died, the last of the Herodians, and his kingdom too was annexed to the province of Syria; even the Decapolis appears to have lost its independent status. By the end of the first century AD Nabataea was the only missing piece in the Roman jigsaw of the Middle East.

If a deal had indeed been struck for a peaceful transfer to Roman rule, it is intriguing to speculate about what Rabbel's heir, Obodas or Malichus, thought of the arrangement. And if there had been such a deal, was it perhaps because they were unfit to rule – the products of generations of sister-marriages? We will probably never know.

What we do know is that in most parts of Rabbel's domains, his people enjoyed peace and prosperity in the final decades of the Nabataean kingdom. In the south, both Petra and Hegra continued to expand. There was great prosperity in the Nabataean-ruled part of Auranitis (present-day Hauran), the fertile hinterland that surrounded Bostra, the main city of the northern Nabataean kingdom. It was an abundant agricultural area, particularly rich in vines, whose motifs can be seen in much of the carved decoration of both pre-Roman and Roman buildings throughout the Hauran; it was also rich in wheat, making it the granary of both Roman Syria and northern Nabataea. Bostra – the focus and meeting point of several northern trade routes, which gained importance as the southern traffic diminished – became Rabbel II's favoured place of residence and, as such, the alternative Nabataean capital. This is reflected in an inscription of AD 93 which refers to the king as 'our lord who is at Bostra'. To make his chosen city more worthy to be the residence of the king, new building projects were put in hand, of which there remain only a handsome arched gate and some column capitals of characteristically simple, but strong, Nabataean design. Whatever else there may have been of Nabataean Bostra was either incorporated as building material in the Roman city that replaced it, or still lies hidden beneath its walls and streets.

Rabbel II's reign ended in AD 106, eight years after Trajan had become Roman emperor. In that year, according to the

PART OF A RELIEF CARVING ON THE FAÇADE OF A BLACK BASALT BUILDING IN THE HAURAN. THE AGRICULTURAL ABUNDANCE OF THE REGION, IN PARTICULAR ITS VINEYARDS, LED TO THE VINE BEING A POPULAR DECORATIVE MOTIF.

historian Cassius Dio, 'Palma the governor of Syria subdued the part of Arabia around Petra and made it subject to the Romans'.[12] It is the only reference we have to the annexation of the Nabataean kingdom and its incorporation as the major part of the new Roman province of Arabia. We do not know if Cornelius Palma led a military expedition into Nabataea but the total absence, in any source, of a recorded furore suggests that he did not need to. Even the Roman coins minted soon after the annexation refer to 'Arabia adquisita', not 'capta' as was inscribed on coins celebrating several other new Roman territories – the Nabataean kingdom had been acquired, not captured.

BOSTRA, IN THE NORTH OF THE
NABATAEAN KINGDOM, WAS
DEVELOPED INTO AN
ALTERNATIVE CAPITAL BY THE
LAST TWO KINGS, MALICHUS II
AND RABBEL II. THOUGH THE
CITY WAS REBUILT BY THE
ROMANS, THIS ARCH AND SOME
CHARACTERISTICALLY PLAIN
'NABATAEAN' CAPITALS, STILL
REMAIN FROM ITS EARLIER DAYS.

QASR AL-BASHIR, ONE OF A STRING OF FORTS THAT THE ROMANS BUILT TO
GUARD THEIR EASTERN FRONTIER. THE BUILDING OF FORTS AND ROADS WERE
AMONG THE MAIN ACTIVITIES OF ROMAN LEGIONARIES IN THE EARLY YEARS OF
THE PROVINCE OF ARABIA.

It was only the top management that changed — the non-resident emperor, resident governors, generals and a few senior officials. Roman legions were now based throughout the erstwhile kingdom and, since there was little fighting to be done, either fort- or road-building, or both, seem to have been their main occupations. Julius Apollinaris, a Roman soldier with the 3rd Cyrenaica legion based at Bostra, wrote to his father in March 107 that his subordinates worked day in day out cutting stones, a task from which his superior rank exempted him — particularly delightful as he had only recently been promoted. A vast quantity of cut stones would have been needed; forts were built at every strategic point in the province, and between AD 111 and 114 the 400-km Via Nova Traiana (Trajan's new road) was constructed all the way from Bostra, via Petra, to Aela (Aqaba) on the Red Sea, following ancient routes. With such a road running the length of the province, the Romans had little difficulty in keeping order among their newly acquired population.

The Nabataean people had almost overnight become subjects of Rome. In due course the royal army was absorbed into the Roman auxiliary forces as six 'Petraean cohorts', a total of 4500-6000 men. As for the non-military majority — landowners, housewives, international traders, local merchants, farmers, stonemasons, ceramicists, scribes, priests, musicians, jugglers or minor officials — most stayed where they were, paid their taxes to the new authority and pursued the accustomed daily pattern of their lives more or less unchanged.

PART OF THE VIA NOVA TRAIANA, THE NEW ROAD BUILT IN AD 111 TO 114 BY THE EMPEROR TRAJAN TO LINK BOSTRA, IN THE NORTH OF THE ROMAN PROVINCE OF ARABIA, WITH PETRA AND THE RED SEA PORT OF AELA (AQABA) IN THE SOUTH.

FIVE

THE MIRACLE
OF PETRA

The Development of
the Capital

enigmatic; but in many ancient cultures snakes represented spirits of the underworld who stood guard over the dead, and there are enough images of snakes in funerary contexts in Petra to suggest that they had a similar role in Nabataean belief.

For the first centuries of the Nabataeans' occupation of Petra, from around the early third to the early first centuries BC, the face of the city probably changed little. Buildings were simple and the main additions would have been tombs with non-figurative decoration whose grandeur varied according to the economic status of the person; and also small wayside niches in honour of one or more of the gods (usually depicted as rectangular blocks). There would have been multiplying flights of steps to reach either their high places of worship and sacrifice, or their installations for water storage and distribution. And more and more inscriptions were carved into the rock faces in the beautiful script that the Nabataeans were evolving from Aramaic, the lingua franca of the ancient Middle East.

During this period, the Siq may have provided the most visible index of change in the Nabataean capital. Increasingly along the full length of its towering penumbra there are votive niches which were carved into the rock walls at different periods throughout the kingdom, transforming it from a merely functional thoroughfare into a numinous sacred way. This continued even after Roman annexation, for some niches and dedications bear a second-century AD date. That the Nabataeans may not have shared the modern world's dichotomy between the practical and the holy is suggested by the recent discovery during excavations in the Siq of reliefs showing two pairs of camels and cameleers, one and a half times life size, carved into one side of the cliff face. They are on either side of a bend in the Siq, facing in towards the angle, as if towards an altar that no longer exists. Whatever their date, these reliefs speak of a city that owed its existence and its abundance to the caravan trade, and to that supreme long-distance haulage vehicle — the camel.

The Siq, the main watercourse between the eastern hills and the heart of the city, must at times have been a terrifying

THE SIQ, HAVING HAD THE DESTRUCTIVE FLOODWATERS DIVERTED AWAY FROM IT, WAS USED FOR THE CONTROLLED CHANNELLING OF WATER INTO THE SOUTH-EAST AREAS OF PETRA; ON THE SOUTH SIDE (LEFT OF PICTURE) THE CHANNEL WAS COVERED WITH SLABS OF STONE, WHILE ON THE NORTH HIGH PRESSURE CERAMIC PIPES WERE LAID INSIDE THE CHANNEL.

THROUGHOUT THE LENGTH OF THE SIQ THE NABATAEANS CARVED NICHES WITH *BETYLS*, RECTANGULAR BLOCKS WHICH REPRESENTED THEIR GODS. WHOEVER COMMISSIONED THIS NICHE, WITH ITS TEN *BETYLS*, APPEARS TO HAVE BEEN HEDGING HIS BETS AS TO WHICH DEITY TO HONOUR.

place in the winters of those early years. From May to October (and often for longer) it would be bone-dry, a tranquil and shaded passage into the city. But once the winter rains began, occasionally falling in torrents, the first cascades would hurtle over the cliffs of the Siq which would soon become a rushing watercourse. Occasionally there would be a devastating flash flood from the downpour on the eastern hills: announced by a crescendoing roar, a wall of water would crash into this natural cleft in the rock, whose narrowness increased the speed and power of the torrent, tossing vast boulders through the channel as though they were pebbles. Any mere human being, or donkey or camel, would be tossed along with them. Doubtless there were tragedies; and the chastened Nabataeans faced the challenge of

how to control, divert and tame the water, to channel and store it, so that it might be used for their benefit rather than for their destruction.

No detail escaped the scrutiny, decision-making and action of these gifted engineers. First they cut a tunnel through a rocky hill near the entrance to the Siq; then they built a dam so that in future flood water would be directed along a subsidiary watercourse that skirts the mountain now known as Jabal al-Khubtha. The main body of this diverted water emerged at the north-east corner of the mountain and, turning west, followed the course of Wadi Mataha which then veered south between high cliffs shortly before reaching the paved street. Here the water was held in a reservoir formed by the construction of a dam wall across the end of the cliffs. At this point beside the street the Nabataeans built their nymphaeum, a fountain house decorated with statues of nymphs that was a basic requirement of all Graeco-Roman cities and was adopted in the oriental world – according to the volume of water in the nymphaeum so the status of a city was assessed.

ONE OF TWO PAIRS OF CAMELS AND CAMELEERS, CARVED ONE AND A HALF
TIMES LIFE SIZE ON A ROCK FACE IN THE SIQ; IT MAY BE AN ACKNOWLEDGEMENT
OF THE ROLE OF THE CAMEL AND THE CARAVAN TRADE IN CREATING THE
WEALTH OF THE NABATAEAN KINGDOM.

But this diversion of the flood waters was only a partial
solution; all along the Siq, side-wadis channelled the winter rains
into this main watercourse, creating further hazards. The
Nabataeans dammed them, not so much for storage as to reduce
the rate of the water's flow for the sake of safety. In gullies too
small to dam, they cut steps to reduce the speed of the water as
it careered down to the Siq; and – also to lower the velocity of
the water – they carefully graded the angle of decline of the road
through the Siq to a regular and gentle five per cent from the
entrance beside the dam to the point, over 1 km later, where it
emerged into an open clearing.

Those were the provisions for winter. In the long summer
months different arrangements were needed, for now the problem was scarcity of water rather than its dangerous excess.
Despite Strabo's assertion that Petra had 'springs in abundance,

tomb — more opulent than our Obelisk Tomb, and built rather than carved into a rock face — which Simon, brother of Judas Maccabeus, commissioned at the family's home town of Modiin near the Mediterranean coast, for another brother, Jonathan, who died in 143 BC; a pyramid represented each of the parents and their five sons: 'He made it high that it might be seen, with polished stone at the front and back. He also erected seven pyramids, opposite one another, for his father and mother and four brothers. And for the pyramids he devised an elaborate setting, erecting about them great columns.'[3]

The Maccabees and their Hasmonaean descendants — in particular Alexander Jannaeus, the contemporary of Obodas I and Aretas III — all borrowed design ideas from the same Hellenistic and other sources as the Nabataeans, and doubtless they also lifted ideas from each other. Tombs that incorporate pyramidal designs are known in Jerusalem from the Iron Age up to the first century AD. We have no means of knowing if the Obelisk Tomb at Petra has any direct relationship with early Jerusalem tombs, or with the Modiin tomb, either in design or date; neither does it have a secure link to the mid-first century AD. Since the area east of the Siq is known to have been the location of Gaia, an early settlement of the Nabataeans (perhaps even their original capital), it would not be surprising to find here some of the earliest Nabataean monuments.

It is perhaps to Aretas III (85-62 BC), the son of Obodas I, that we can attribute the most famous of all the monuments of Petra — the Khazneh, or Treasury — though some scholars date it to nearer the end of the first century BC and the reign of Aretas IV. The absense of inscriptions makes any dating speculative. Whoever commissioned it, it is hard to escape the conclusion that this spectacular and elaborately carved façade was designed with the intention to impress and to overawe anyone, Nabataean and foreigner alike, who entered the city by this route. After the long and haunted twilight of the Siq comes the sudden brilliance of this astonishing monument. While the

THE KHAZNEH (TREASURY), THE MOST FAMOUS AND ELABORATELY CARVED OF ALL THE FAÇADES OF PETRA, STILL PRESENTS PUZZLES REGARDING ITS DATE, WHO COMMISSIONED IT, AND ITS PURPOSE; BUT THE WEALTH OF FUNERARY SYMBOLS IN ITS DECORATION SUGGESTS THAT IT WAS ASSOCIATED WITH THE NABATAEAN CULT OF THE DEAD.

international traders may have become accustomed to the architectural styles and figurative ornamentation of other cultures, the average stay-at-home Nabataeans must have been astounded to see the shapes and decorative motifs of this new and unorthodox monument being released from the confining rock. Nothing in their previous experience could have prepared them for it. At that stage, not only was no other monument in Petra so vast, but the Nabataeans were used to their gods being portrayed as simple rectangular blocks of carved stone, a stern and uncluttered representation that fitted well with a people of ascetic nomadic origins. Add to this the fact that the ground level in front of the Khazneh was then about four metres lower than it is today, enhancing the drama of this strange new monument as it unfolded high above the heads of passers-by.

At first it may have been simply its size that astonished the fascinated onlookers. As the basic outline emerged from under the masons' chisels, and shapeless lumps were left to be refined later into a pediment or a capital or a frieze, it may have seemed that, despite the new monument's unprecedented scale, they were still in the non-figurative world in which they felt at home. But then a profusion of human shapes emerged, and Nabataean and Greek deities, as well as characters from Greek mythology, began to people the bays and recesses of the new façade. Though the figures are now somewhat eroded, and some were vandalized by ancient iconoclasts, we see on either side of the lower order, each standing beside a horse, the Dioscuri — the heavenly twins Castor and Pollux, who guided the souls of the dead to the Elysian Fields. Above them, in the upper order, are Amazons wielding axes, winged Victories, a Medusa head, griffins and eagles. All are funerary symbols.

Presiding over this eclectic band, at the centre of the tholos (the round section at the top of the façade) stands a female figure carrying a cornucopia — an attribute of Tyche, Greek goddess of fortune and the protection of cities. The acroterion at the apex of the pediment below, set like a badge at the foot of the goddess's pedestal, bears the device of Isis, supreme goddess of the Egyptian pantheon who, as the consort of Osiris, ruled the underworld and the spirits of the dead. Isis was commonly identified with both Tyche and the Greek goddess of love, Aphrodite; and Aphrodite was identified with the Nabataean al-'Uzza, great goddess of Petra. This single figure, protectress of the city and goddess of love and of immortality, represents a host of divine assimilations from the contemporary world of the Nabataeans. Encompassing all these figures, on friezes and

THE FRIEZE OF LEAVES AND FRUITS ON THE UPPER ORDER OF THE KHAZNEH; THE HUMAN FACE IN THE CENTRE WAS VANDALIZED IN ANTIQUITY.

BETWEEN THE COLUMNS AT THE CENTRE OF THE CIRCULAR THOLOS AT THE TOP OF THE KHAZNEH STANDS A GODDESS CARRYING A CORNUCOPIA, A COMPOSITE REPRESENTATION OF AL-'UZZA/APHRODITE/TYCHE; AND THE CARVED BADGE AT HER FEET BEARS THE DEVICE OF YET ANOTHER IDENTIFICATION — ISIS.

capitals and in the pediment, are finely carved vases, rosettes, flowers, leaves, fronds and fruit, much of it still extraordinarily well preserved.

While conservative members of Petra's population may have been disturbed at this wholesale abandonment of their ancient non-figurative tradition, it does not appear to have been an infringement of Nabataean religious laws. Far from dying away, figurative art — particularly the carving of fruits and flowers and real or mythical animals — multiplied all over Petra; and

mythological characters, and foreign counterparts of the gods, continued to be portrayed in human shape, alongside their more traditional block-like forms. For most Nabataeans these carvings on the Khazneh must have been regarded as nothing more than exotic decoration, to be admired or criticized simply on the basis of aesthetic taste, and were not considered to be in conflict with the real objects of their worship.

This image of the idyllic world of the gods is potently influenced, both in its iconography and in its architectural details, by the contemporary Hellenistic world whose creative centre and capital was Alexandria. Structural and design ideas that had originated in Greece in the fifth or fourth centuries BC took on in Alexandria new and individual forms. The capitals of the Khazneh, with their acanthus bases and entwined fronds and flowers, are closely related to those of second- and first-century BC Alexandria, themselves adaptations of the classic Corinthian style. Both the broken pediment at the top of the Khazneh, and the round tholos in the centre with its tent-like roof, were architectural features known in Hellenistic Alexandria; and both appear in Pompeii's Second-Style wall paintings (three-dimensional architectural representations that could realistically be built), for which Alexandria also provided the inspiration. It is thought that Alexandrian craftsmen may have been brought to Petra to work on this façade and to train local sculptors and masons to carve the designs they used. But this is no slavish copy of a Greek original; here Hellenistic ideas were brilliantly transformed into a work of art that kept a distinctively Nabataean flavour.

It is only in our mind's eye that we can recreate the Khazneh in its original glory, when the natural courtyard in front of it, four metres below the present ground level and enclosed within sheer russet-coloured cliffs, was splendidly paved with large hexagonal limestone slabs. The multitude of ancient dams and water channels in all the clefts of the rocks that surround the court suggest that their purpose may have been to supply water for an abundant pool or water garden. And high above this enclosed aqueous paradise, carved into the western cliff, soared this breathtaking monument.

One thing that is certain about the Khazneh is that it was not, in fact, a treasury. Its full Arabic name, Khaznet Far'oun[4] (Pharaoh's Treasury), relates to a folktale which identified this façade with mythical treasure deposited in the crowning urn by a wicked and fabulously wealthy magician — reputed to be none other than the Pharaoh who drove Moses and his followers out of Egypt and chased them here to Wadi Mousa, the Valley of Moses. On the assumption that a Pharaoh would inevitably take all the wealth of Egypt on his travels, it appears that by the time he reached Petra the Pharaonic treasure had become such an impediment that it had to be offloaded. Where else would it be put except in the most lavishly carved of all the monuments? Problems of chronology — such as the Khazneh being carved nearly 1200 years after the supposed time of Moses — evidently did not impinge on the myth.

Theories abound as to the Khazneh's real function, so far with no secure resolution; but from the wealth of funerary symbolism in its carvings, it was clearly connected with the Nabataean cult of the dead, and its grandeur indicates a royal patron. If it was indeed made for Aretas III, it might have been either as his own tomb or as a memorial mausoleum dedicated to his father, the deified Obodas I. The lack of burial slots seems to favour the second option, for Obodas is said to have been buried in the Negev, at the town that took its name from him — Oboda. The Khazneh's strong Hellenistic overtones certainly fit well with the king whose epithet, Philhellene, proclaimed his love of Greek culture; and the multifaceted preoccupation with immortality throughout its carved decoration suggests a cult of a ruler who had joined the ranks of the immortals.

While Aretas III had some breaks in his military programme which could have been filled with construction projects, his two immediate successors may have had fewer such opportunities. The shadowy Obodas II reigned only two years, while Malichus I was recurrently involved in wars for or against the

INSIDE THE PORTICO OF THE KHAZNEH CARVED PORTALS LEAD INTO SMALL ROOMS, PERHAPS GUARD ROOMS, ON EITHER SIDE OF THE STEPS THAT LEAD UP TO THE MAIN CHAMBER.

Romans, the machinations of Cleopatra and conflict with Herod the Great. It is probably only with the accession of Obodas III in 30 BC, which coincided with the emergence of Augustus as Roman *princeps*, that the Pax Romana brought sufficient peace in the region to allow the Nabataeans to spend time on the glorification of their capital. This found its full expression in the long and largely peaceful reign of Obodas III's heir, Aretas IV, 'who loves his people', another possible creator of Khazneh.

Over a century after the Khazneh was carved it provided the model for two other carved monuments – one of the Royal Tombs in the western face of Jabal al-Khubtha and the vast façade high in the mountains known as ad-Deir, the Monastery. The former, the Corinthian Tomb, acquired its name from an early visitor to Petra, the French aristocrat Léon de Laborde, who came here in 1828 and, with the classicizing tendency of his time and caste, described it as 'a monument of the Corinthian order.' In fact, the capitals are of the neo-Corinthian style developed in Alexandria, and both they and the whole façade appear to be a half-hearted repetition of some of the Khazneh's designs, but with an arched pediment over the entrance and, between the lower and upper orders, a row of dwarf columns and capitals and a broken pediment. The tomb is now badly eroded, which does not favour it in any comparison with its better-preserved model, but rather highlights its squatter, less aesthetic proportions and the inferiority of its carving. It is as though the craftsmen who made it could no longer summon up enthusiasm for the exotic design and ornamentation that had been so revolutionary, and so beautifully realized, in the Khazneh.

THE ERODED CORINTHIAN TOMB, SO CALLED BECAUSE A NINETEENTH CENTURY TRAVELLER, LÉON DE LABORDE, THOUGHT ITS CAPITALS WERE OF THE CORINTHIAN ORDER. THE DESIGN OF THE TOMB REFLECTS THAT OF THE KHAZNEH, THOUGH ITS PROPORTIONS ARE LESS AESTHETIC AND THE CARVING INFERIOR.

In the Deir we find a closer similarity to the overall design of the Khazneh, with its tholos and broken pediment and no additional level between the two orders – and, in the hands of more skilled designers and craftsmen than those who executed the Corinthian Tomb, the result is one of the most original and harmonious of Nabataean façades. The scale of the Deir is prodigious, dwarfing to ant size the human beings who stand before it today, as it did those who carved it from the rock 2000 years ago. The niches, evidently created to hold statues of kings, or of gods in human form, now stand empty, and all the other decoration – the lovely, simple Doric frieze of alternating triglyphs (three vertical rectangles) and circular metopes, and the uncluttered column capitals – is rigorously non-figurative. It is as though the Nabataean stonemasons, having seen the plain

THE DEIR (MONASTERY) AS DRAWN BY DAVID ROBERTS RA IN THE EARLY NINETEENTH CENTURY. THE ROCK-CUT TEMPLE, FROM WHOSE TERRACE HE MADE THIS DRAWING, CAN STILL BE SEEN, COMPLETE WITH A FINELY CARVED SACRED NICHE AT THE BACK AND THE SCANTY REMAINS OF A ROW OF COLUMNS ACROSS ITS FRONT.

THE DEIR (MONASTERY) CARVED INTO THE HONEY-COLOURED SANDSTONE OF JABAL AD-DEIR NORTH-WEST OF THE HEART OF PETRA. LIKE THE CORINTHIAN TOMB, IT WAS MODELLED ON THE KHAZNEH, THOUGH STRIPPED OF 'FOREIGN' FIGURATIVE CARVING. ONE OF THE LARGEST — YET ALSO ONE OF THE MOST HARMONIOUS — OF PETRA'S CARVED FAÇADES, ITS SCALE DWARFS HUMAN BEINGS. IT MAY HAVE BEEN USED FOR MEMORIAL FEASTS IN HONOUR OF THE GOD-KING OBODAS I.

A VAST STONE URN, SET ON TOP OF A NABATAEAN CAPITAL, CROWNS THE DEIR.

Above PART OF THE DORIC FRIEZE AT THE TOP OF THE DEIR, WITH UNADORNED CIRCULAR METOPES ALTERNATING WITH TRIGLYPHS, GROUPS OF THREE VERTICAL RECTANGLES LIKE MINIATURE COLUMNS.

shapes that were blocked out of the stone prior to carving an elaborate Alexandrian-style floral capital, decided that the blocked out form was stronger and more beautiful and more in keeping with the Nabataean ethos. With this plain 'Nabataean' capital any kind of figurative decoration would have looked out of place.

The scale of the Deir, the long uphill sweep of the grand processional way that leads to it, the remains of a colonnaded courtyard in front of it and of a vast circular structure just beyond – all point to a monument of special significance. Recent clearance work inside the chamber has revealed that this was a triclinium; and an inscription nearby, found in the early twentieth century, may indicate the person in whose honour the memorial feasts were held here: 'Let be remembered 'Ubaydu son of Waqihel and his associates of the symposium of Obodas the god.' The deified Obodas died around 85 BC but, if the inscription does relate to this monument, his cult clearly still flourished well over a century later, for the Deir is believed to have been carved in the mid-first century AD.

Although figurative façades continued to be carved in Petra, most Nabataean architectural forms appear to have developed from the elaborate to the simple, from the figurative to the aniconic – from the Khazneh to the Deir – a reversal of what is generally assumed. In another of the Royal Tombs, the Urn

THE ORNATELY CARVED TOMB OF SEXTIUS FLORENTINUS, ONE OF THE EARLY ROMAN GOVERNORS OF THE PROVINCE OF ARABIA, WHO DIED C.AD 129 AND WAS BURIED AT HIS OWN REQUEST IN PETRA.

A PLAIN NABATAEAN CAPITAL, SHOWING AN INSET PIECE OF STONE ON THE LEFT-HAND 'HORN', PERHAPS TO PUT RIGHT A SLIP OF THE CHISEL. THE MEND WOULD HAVE BEEN MASKED BY THE PLASTER AND PAINT WITH WHICH IT WAS COVERED.

Tomb, and also in the non-royal Roman Soldier Tomb in Wadi Farasa (which despite its name is Nabataean), human figures, presumably the occupants of the tomb, are in an otherwise strictly non-figural framework. And even where complex designs were used – such as in the huge and extravagant Palace Tomb and the Bab as-Siq Triclinium – floral and other figurative elements were eliminated in favour of the non-representational. A notable exception is the Tomb of Sextius Florentinus, one of the few monuments to have a clear date, since this Roman governor of the province of Arabia is known to have died around AD 129. At his own request he was buried here in Petra in a slightly out-of-the-way spot just around a curve in the mountain from the impressive range of the Royal Tombs – a modesty perhaps forced on him by the Nabataean kings having already taken all the grandest locations. His tomb is also noticeably smaller than those of the kings, but what it lacks in size it makes up for in ornamentation. Here we are back in the world of classical ideas adapted to Nabataean vision; there is a (probable) Medusa head beneath the arched pediment and an eagle above it, unadorned 'Nabataean' capitals, and a Latin inscription dedicating the tomb to Titus Aninius Sextius Florentinus.

So far we have mostly looked at 'royal' monuments. But the vast majority of Petra's tombs were carved for ordinary citizens whose wide-ranging economic status is indicated by their varying sizes, and the quality of the carving. The most popular designs for richer members of society are today called the Proto-Hegra and the Hegra styles because of their similarity to most of the tombs at Hegra. The former has a simple cavetto cornice beneath a pair of monumental Assyrian crowsteps, while the latter also has a classical cornice, frieze and architrave below this. Both frequently had engaged pilasters with Nabataean capitals on either side of the lower half; and often, but not always, there was a classical-style doorway in the middle, with subsidiary pilasters and capitals, sometimes with a pediment above it.

One such Hegra-style tomb at Petra (tomb no. 825) has been studied in great detail in recent years with the ultimate purpose of learning how best to preserve these increasingly fragile monuments. Some fascinating information has emerged about how the Nabataean stonemasons carved the façades in the sandstone cliffs. It was already known – from several unfinished façades in various parts of Petra – that the work started from the top. First the natural rock face would have a smoothly dressed recess cut into it, just larger than the planned monument, and then the detailed carving began, with the masons working from top to bottom. They could have been let down by ropes, or climbed up rickety wooden scaffolding, or they may have cut a ledge in the rock, wide enough for them to move on freely, which became lower and lower as they carved their way down the façade.

At least four different types of tool have been identified as having been used. One of them, a basic pickaxe, was already known from an incised rock drawing by an ancient Nabataean – presumably a mason identifying his trade. Such a tool was used where a rough finish was adequate, in areas such as the tops of cornices and pediments that could not be seen by people on the ground. A pointed chisel might also have been used in other areas where a rough finish would do, such as where pieces of stone had to be inset to replace damaged or poor-quality areas of the base rock. Either this pointed chisel or – more likely – a toothed chisel would have been used to create the surface parallel lines that are so characteristic a feature of Nabataean architecture. Depending on what was to be superimposed on this grooved surface, the parallel lines were angled at between 15° and 45° from the vertical. For even finer work, often bordering areas of diagonal grooving, a flat chisel was used.

Traces of plaster still cling to the cut surfaces in several areas of tomb 825, indicating that the whole façade was plastered, and then almost certainly painted. Remains of wall paintings in other monuments in Petra indicate that the Nabataeans painted both their carved façades and their buildings, using bold sections of strong colour, particularly deep reds and yellows, in an apparent unwillingness to accept the extraordinary palette that nature had imposed upon them. The plaster would also have protected the soft sandstone and hidden any underlying imperfections. Indeed, it is very revealing to see how the Nabataeans covered up areas of poor stone — and sometimes poor workmanship — by cutting recesses in the rock, into which they put extraneous stone which was then carved in the same pattern as the base rock. Later, when ceramic water pipes were set into the northern wall of the Siq, and on into the heart of the city, these masking techniques once more came into their own to hide the groove that had been cut right across the face of this tomb, and the inset pipes that were held in place with small stones and mortar. Careful plastering and painting would have completely hidden the pipes from view.

Above and beside the tomb the masons carved a network of channels to direct rainwater away from the façade, so reducing the risk of damage to the plaster and paint and to the rock itself. Most of the damage caused to this and other façades has come from water cascading down the front in the centuries since the water channels became blocked.

As for the masons' sources of inspiration — on two areas of smoothed rock beside the tomb we can see incised profiles of a cornice, presumably executed by the master-stonemason as guidance for the workmen executing that particular feature — what is more, the incised profiles and the finished cornice profiles actually match. And alongside one of these profiles is an incised outline of a rectangular block — the representation of the god Dushara, perhaps as an artisan's dedication of the work in progress to the great god.

If today Petra looks like a vast and rather grand ancient cemetery, in the period of the Nabataean kingdom, and into the Roman and Byzantine eras, it was primarily a place for the living. With houses, temples and public buildings occupying the heart of the city, the magnificent tombs, carved into the surrounding mountains, would not then have been as dominant as they are today when so little of the fabric of the ancient city still stands to any great height. Buildings, even the most imposing temples, are naturally more susceptible to earthquakes than are carved façades. As more of these buildings are excavated, and released from their deep layers of dust and wind-blown earth, so

we will more easily be able to imagine the structure of the thriving urban community that once inhabited this place.

At some time in the early first century BC, the simple buildings beside the watercourse were levelled to create a terrace on which was laid the first street worthy of the name — a sand and gravel road almost 18 metres wide, bordered with columns and porticoes and buildings of fine ashlar masonry. From the point

THE COLONNADED STREET AT THE HEART OF PETRA, OVERLOOKED ON THE EAST BY THE ROYAL TOMBS, CARVED INTO JABAL AL-KHUBTHA. THE STREET WAS THE FOCUS OF THE CITY'S PUBLIC LIFE, THE REFERENCE POINT FOR THE GRID SYSTEM ON WHICH THE TEMPLES AND OTHER PUBLIC BUILDINGS WERE CONSTRUCTED.

where Wadi Mataha brought the diverted Siq waters to the main wadi and where the nymphaeum was built, down to the Arched Gate at the western end, the colonnaded street became the focus of the city's public life. Like other cities of the period, Petra now had a grand ceremonial street of which its citizens could be proud. It was not a thoroughfare for it led nowhere; rather, it was literally an end of the road for people coming in from the east.

The colonnaded street provided the basic reference point for the Hippodamian grid on which many of the splendid new temples and other public buildings were constructed. These were reached through the Arched Gate to the west, two stairways on the south, and bridges spanning the watercourse on the north. At some uncertain point in the first century AD, the gravel road may have been replaced by stone paving, laid along the same line.

Previous pages QASR AL-BINT, THE MAIN TEMPLE OF PETRA; IN FRONT OF IT ARE
THE REMAINS OF AN ALTAR, AND BETWEEN THIS AND THE ARCHED GATE LIES
THE LONG, NARROW TEMENOS, OR SACRED PRECINCT IN WHICH WORSHIPPERS
GATHERED.

Noticeably not on the alignment of the street — and built
beyond the end of it — is the temple known as Qasr al-Bint. This
is an abbreviation of its full Arabic name, Qasr al-Bint Far'oun
(the palace of Pharaoh's daughter), which again relates to a local
folktale, this time about the virtuous daughter of the same
wicked Pharaoh of the Khazneh, who set a test for would-be
suitors to bring water to her palace. Of the two who completed
the task simultaneously, from different springs in the hills, the
princess chose the more modest suitor who ascribed his success
to God as well as to his own prowess.

Far from being a palace, or having any relationship with a
Pharaoh, Qasr al-Bint is a Nabataean temple, possibly the main
temple of Petra. It stands beneath the rock of al-Habees at the
western limit of a long walled and paved temenos, or sacred
precinct, which ran from the end of the colonnaded street
between the watercourse and the southern slope of the Petra
basin. The temple was built in the first century BC, perhaps in the
time of Obodas III, apparently replacing an earlier version. This
solid-looking, four-square temple, built of russet sandstone ashlar blocks, is the only one of Petra's built monuments to have
survived almost intact the recurrent earthquakes that toppled the
other buildings. But the four huge columns, which stood across
the entrance in front of the soaring arch that leads into the temple, did fall. These columns once carried capitals, probably similar in style to those of the Khazneh; and laid on top of the capitals was a horizontal entablature, decorated with a handsome
Doric frieze, which extended all the way round the top of the
building. Originally the circular elements in the frieze, the
metopes, contained large open flowers alternating with human
busts; but now none of the busts remains in situ, apparently the
result of replacement or defacing in a non-figurative reworking
in antiquity. One bust was found some years ago in a dump near
the Arched Gate. The walls, both inside and out, were completely covered with panels of decorative plasterwork mimicking
stone carving, some of which can still be seen on the outside
walls. Inside only small fragments survive, but the walls are
pocked with holes which once held the all-covering plaster in
place. And the plaster was painted in the strong colours that the

THE DORIC FRIEZE THAT RUNS ALONG THE TOP OF QASR AL-BINT ORIGINALLY
HAD BUSTS OF GODS ALTERNATING WITH ROSETTES; IN A LATER REMODELLING,
THE BUSTS WERE REPLACED WITH MORE ROSETTES.

Nabataeans favoured. With colours such as these, Petra would to
most modern eyes have appeared extremely gaudy.

Worshippers would have entered the temenos through the
Arched Gate at the end of the street, and made their way to the
large open altar where sacrifices were offered by the priests in
honour of the god whose statue stood at the back of the temple
opposite. In 1959 the British archaeologist Peter Parr found
a gigantic marble hand inside the temple, part of a cultic statue
that must have stood at least six metres high in the cella, or holy
of holies, in the central chamber at the back of the sanctuary.
The evidence is somewhat confusing as to which god was

worshipped here. Though it might seem odd if so important a temple were not, at least originally, dedicated to Dushara, no Nabataean inscription has been found here, nor any reference to Dushara. But there are two dedications in Greek from the Roman period: one to Aphrodite (identified with al-'Uzza, the supreme goddess of Petra); the other to 'Zeus *hypsistos*' (most high), with which particular epithet of Zeus the Syrian god Ba'al-Shamin was more usually identified than the Nabataean Dushara. This may indicate that the temple had a double dedication – to al-'Uzza/Aphrodite and to Ba'al-Shamin/Zeus.

Some years (or decades) after the completion of Qasr al-Bint, a new temple was begun on the slopes north of the main street. As if to prove that the Nabataeans had no rigid rules for the design of their temples and were open to new architectural ideas, this temple – today called the Temple of the Winged Lions – presents a quite different architectural style. An entrance portico leads into the cella, in which a raised altar platform is surrounded by a forest of columns; most of the capitals, with their entwined fronds and flowers, greatly resemble those of the Khazneh and Qasr al-Bint. The columns nearest the altar had lively winged lions in place of the volutes of the capitals, and this unusual feature has given the building its modern name. They are no longer in situ. In its first form, the temple was lavishly plastered with decorative cornices and other mouldings, and some of the columns were covered with elaborate stucco designs. The plaster was then painted with delicate floral and foliate motifs, human busts, chalices and dolphins – a visual feast for those with tendencies towards ornamentation.

The excavations, conducted since 1974 by an American team led by Dr Philip Hammond, have uncovered not only the temple itself, but also crypts, annexes and living quarters adjoining it on the west. Three artisans' workshops were found here, evidently for the upkeep of the temple and for vital running repairs. One studio was for painters – ceramic bowls, funnels

The Temple of the Winged Lions, with its forest of columns surrounding a raised altar, stands on the slope to the north of the Colonnaded street. On the opposite slope is the Great temple.

and other vessels were found in it, some of the smaller bowls still containing the pigments used to touch up the wall paintings inside the temple. Another studio was for metal workers, and the third for marble carvers.

In the marble carvers' workshop an almost complete dedicatory inscription was found, precisely dated to 'the 4th day of 'Ab, the 37th year of Aretas, king of the Nabataeans, who loves his people' – this refers to Aretas IV in August AD 27, incidentally, just about the time that his daughter was being divorced by Herod Antipas. The inscription may date to the temple's initial building, or perhaps to a later remodelling when the original elaborate frescos and mouldings were completely plastered over. This appears to have been done deliberately to reduce the ornamentation – the exotic elements in Nabataean monuments – and to revert to the plainer, more traditional style with which many Nabataeans clearly felt more at ease.

One of the most extraordinary and beautiful Nabataean cultic images was discovered in a niche in the cella of the Temple of the Winged Lions – a small rectangular block of stone with almond-shaped eye recesses beneath prominent brows, a long straight nose and oval mouth, all carved within a simple border. It is pure Nabataean in style, with no Hellenistic influence, the stylized features the only concession to an anthropomorphic representation of a god. Above the brows runs a foliate headband with a carefully carved indentation in the centre which is presumed to have held a semiprecious stone engraved with the device of the deity. Tantalizingly, the identity is uncertain since the Nabataean inscription at the bottom offers nothing more revealing than 'the goddess of Hayyan, son of Nybat'. One clue lies in a ceramic votive figurine found in the temple, representing the Egyptian goddess Isis in an attitude of grief,[5] and a statuette of her consort Osiris; another is seen in a less elaborately carved stone with stylized eyes and a headband with the Isis device carved into it. Perhaps, then, the missing device from the

THE 'GODDESS OF HAYYAN SON OF NYBAT', FROM THE TEMPLE OF THE WINGED LIONS, PROBABLY REPRESENTS AL-'UZZA, THE GREAT GODDESS OF PETRA, IDENTIFIED WITH BOTH APHRODITE AND ISIS. IN THE MIDDLE OF HER HEADBAND THERE MAY HAVE BEEN A SEMI-PRECIOUS STONE ENGRAVED WITH THE DEVICE OF ISIS. (PETRA MUSEUM)

headband of the nameless goddess was that of Isis. If so, her identification with the Greek Aphrodite, and Aphrodite's assimilation with al-'Uzza, would suggest that this temple was dedicated to the great goddess of Petra in her identification with Isis, either alone, or jointly with Dushara identified with Osiris.

Around the same time as Qasr al-Bint was built, or a little after, the Nabataeans began another huge project south of the colonnaded street – it has been excavated since 1993 by an American team from Brown University under the direction of Dr Martha Sharp Joukowsky. From a once undulating hillside, with a few fallen columns arranged with natural artistry like spokes of a petrified Catherine wheel, the excavators have gradually revealed the structure, as well as something of the architectural history, of this unique and enigmatic building.

First a spacious terrace was levelled, into which an elaborate system of water channels was laid, for both supply and drainage; and a stone stairway was built up the slope from the street to the middle of the northern edge of the terrace. A great building was erected on the terrace, possibly with two exterior walls with an ambulatory between them – though the outer wall may have been added later. Across the northern front four columns stood between the inner side walls which, at the southern end, were joined by another wall that defined the back of the building. Inside this inner wall rose eight columns along each side, with four columns standing between them at the back and, near the front, two piers on either side of two columns, set immediately behind the four great columns of the façade. At the top of each

THE GREAT TEMPLE ON THE SLOPE TO THE NORTH OF THE COLONNADED STREET. THIS SPECTACULAR BUILDING WAS STARTED IN THE FIRST CENTURY BC AND COMPLETELY REDESIGNED IN THE FOLLOWING CENTURY WITH A THEATRE AT ITS HEART.

AN EARLY FIRST CENTURY AD CARVING FROM PETRA, THOUGHT TO REPRESENT A LAUREL-CROWNED MELPOMENE, THE MUSE OF TRAGEDY, HOLDING A MASK EITHER OF PAN OR A SATYR – PERHAPS AN INDICATION OF THE TYPE OF PERFORMANCE GIVEN IN THE MAIN THEATRE. (AMMAN ARCHAEOLOGICAL MUSEUM)

locating it on the edge of the necropolis and slicing off the façades of a number of tombs. Presumably the tombs were sufficiently old to eliminate the risk of a riot by distressed relatives. The American excavator, Philip Hammond, concluded that the theatre was made in the reign of Aretas IV, whose love for his people clearly extended to giving them a splendid place for entertainment and the fulfilment of their cultural needs. It has also been suggested that the enthusiastic theatre-building activities of Herod the Great, who died early in Aretas' reign, may have urged the Nabataean king to do likewise. Some minor alterations were made to the theatre in the time of Aretas' son and heir, Malichus II; and in the Roman period there was more refurbishment, perhaps necessitated by the earthquake of AD 113/114.

This theatre, though conforming precisely to the rules specified by Vitruvius for the shape, proportions, orientation and stage design of a Roman theatre, and for achieving the best acoustics, was made in true Nabataean style by being cut out of the rock rather than built. The floral capitals, too, are distinctively Nabataean. The achievement is impressive – to trace a semicircle on a convoluted rock face, using nothing more sophisticated than a length of string and a few simple tools, shows a

confident grasp of geometry; and to expend months, or more likely years, hollowing out the rock face with slogging, stone-chipping craftsmanship is extraordinary. To ensure that the theatre did not become a lake when the winter rains fell, an effective, and characteristically Nabataean, system of drainage channels was cut above and around the theatre, diverting the water into cisterns.

In contrast with the very high quality of workmanship of its public buildings, the few houses of Petra that have so far been excavated are markedly more careless in their construction. The mastery of architectural techniques clearly did not filter down to the domestic level. On the slopes above Qasr al-Bint and the Great Temple — an area known as az-Zantur — several houses have been excavated, some with Roman-period buildings above earlier ones from the time of the Nabataean kingdom. In some places excavation has reached the earliest occupation levels, before houses were built at all, with levelled earth floors which were clearly bases for tents. What seems to have happened is that when the transition was made from tent to stone house, the owner would use the original floor space. While he dug good foundations, he paid little attention to making the site more

THE MAIN THEATRE OF PETRA, CARVED OUT OF A HILLSIDE IN THE REIGN OF ARETAS IV (9 BC – AD 40) TO SEAT AN AUDIENCE OF ABOUT 5000 PEOPLE. THE NABATAEANS CARVED WATER CHANNELS ALL AROUND THE TOP OF THE THEATRE TO PREVENT IT BECOMING FLOODED IN THE WINTER RAINS — AS HAPPENED IN MARCH 1991, AFTER WHICH THE CHANNELS WERE CLEARED OF THE ACCUMULATED SILT OF CENTURIES.

secure with retaining walls, and in time some of the house walls bulged or collapsed.

An inevitable result of this haphazard growth of domestic buildings was that there was no formal plan in the residential areas of Petra. The public and official buildings in the lower sections of the city may have been organized on the rectangular Hippodamian grid system so prevalent in the Hellenistic world, but the houses that surrounded them were built at every uncoordinated angle imaginable. As the Swiss excavator, Dr Rolf Stucky, has vividly described it,[7] the living quarters of Petra resembled a petrified nomads' camp — a charmingly irregular setting for the finely worked symmetry at the heart of the city.

A Nabataean house on the southern slopes of Petra. While public monuments in the heart of the city were finely built on a grid system, the houses were at whatever angle suited the terrain or the owner's whim; and building standards were less rigorous.

Inside the houses the floors were paved with flagstones, some rectangular, others hexagonal, and yet others in elaborate *opus sectile* work; and in the grander villas some rooms and courtyards have columns with carved capitals. Most striking of all was the discovery in 1996 of a house with spectacular polychrome frescos. The paintings are a kind of *trompe-l'oeil*, intended to give the illusion of a highly stylized form of architecture, with columned building wings appearing to stand out from the background wall, each panel of which was painted in a different geometrical design. The architectural ideas are similar, but not identical, to some of the carved façades of Petra's tombs, in particular the Khazneh; they are also reminiscent of the second-style Pompeian wall paintings. Above the frescos is elaborate stucco work mimicking masonry, and this enhances the three-dimensional effect of the paintings. The work has provisionally been dated to the early first century AD.

These frescos are the most complex and best-preserved to have been found so far in Petra's residential areas. Of the houses excavated on the Zantur slopes, it is the only one to be so lavishly painted. If the house was of exceptional status, then we would not expect many similar finds; if not, it could be an exciting foretaste of what may be revealed as more houses are excavated. Another painted room has long been known, inside a rock-cut chamber in Wadi Siyyagh; its columned architectural panels resemble the Zantur paintings, but there is nothing of the latter's perspective and three-dimensional effect.

A third painted room is in a completely different style. It is in an area known as al-Beidha – 'the white one', from the pale colour of its rocks – about 3 km north of Petra which, in the early first century AD, was developed as the capital's northern

An architectural *trompe l'oeil* fresco, probably of the first century AD, in a Nabataean house in Petra. The way in which the columned building wings appear to stand out from the background wall is reminiscent of the second-style frescoes from Pompeii.

THE CARVED FAÇADE AT THE ENTRANCE TO SIQ AL-BARID (THE COLD GORGE), A NATURAL CARAVANSERAI IN THE ROCK IN PETRA'S NORTHERN COMMERCIAL SUBURB. HERE TRADING CARAVANS WOULD STAY FOR A FEW DAYS, OUTSIDE THE CITY CENTRE, EN ROUTE BETWEEN THE ARABIAN PENINSULA AND THE MEDITERRANEAN COAST.

commercial suburb. If the trading caravans once went into the heart of Petra, there must have come a point in the great burst of population expansion and urban development from the first century BC onwards when it was deemed no longer practicable or desirable – either for the residents of Petra or for the traders themselves – for this practice to continue. Al-Beidha was already the main entry and exit point for the trade routes to the north, north-west and west – here the caravans from the Negev, Gaza and Ashkelon, from Jerusalem and the Phoenician coast, would settle for a while to engage in trade, their camels and donkeys quartered in al-Beidha's broad and fertile acres. The merchants themselves probably stayed in the cool seclusion of the Siq al-Barid, the cold gorge, a natural caravanserai hidden in the honey-coloured rocks, where they carved a temple, dormitories, cisterns and places of worship. There were triclinia in abundance – large ones, carved in an imposing row – but with no apparent funerary connection for there are no tombs; their clear function was

INSIDE THE FIRST NATURAL COURTYARD OF SIQ AL-BARID THE NABATAEANS CARVED WHAT MAY HAVE BEEN A TEMPLE IN THE ROCK FACE, FOR THE USE OF TRADERS AS THEY STAYED FOR A FEW DAYS EN ROUTE BETWEEN THE ARABIAN PENINSULA AND THE MEDITERRANEAN COAST.

SIX

THE DELICATE
MAGIC OF LIFE

Nabataean Gods and
Places of Worship

ATARGATIS, THE 'SYRIAN GODDESS', WHO WAS WORSHIPPED AT KHIRBET AT-TANNUR TOGETHER WITH THE EDOMITE GOD QOS, WHOSE ATTRIBUTE OF AN EAGLE WITH OUTSPREAD WINGS STANDS OVER HER HEAD. HER ROLE AS GODDESS OF VEGETATION IS INDICATED BY THE CARVED FLOWERS THAT SURROUND HER, AND THE LEAVES GROWING FROM HER FACE AND NECK. (AMMAN ARCHAEOLOGICAL MUSEUM.)

I*n the dust where we have buried the silent races and their abominations, we have buried so much of the delicate magic of life.*

D. H. LAWRENCE

We cannot inhabit any other person's deepest beliefs, primordial fears or perceptions of the divine. We can only — and with the gentlest humility after a gap of 2000 years — guess at those of the Nabataeans. Things that may seem crepuscular to us, or even filled with impenetrable darkness, were clearly for them a source of radiance. Like all human beings, the Nabataeans were seeking explanations for the inexplicable in life, and the manner in which they articulated their quest gives a vivid, if partial, insight into their complex relationships with their immemorial gods.

These deities had no names. The 'names' we know for them are simple expressions of a function, a characteristic or a location, a careful avoidance of a name, an epithet which defines a single comprehensible aspect of a multifaceted and incomprehensible divinity. How can we name a god whom we do not comprehend? And what imagery should we choose? Should we create god in our own image? The Nabataeans adopted a rectangular block, or *betyl*, sometimes carved in relief, sometimes free-standing — a modest recognition of the impossibility of representing the unrepresentable. Yet this block of stone was for them the very abode of the god's presence, and so an object of great sanctity. It was a concept that they shared with many of their neighbours — even the Jewish patriarch Jacob had put up a 'stone, which… shall be God's house';[1] but by the time of the Nabataeans, a prohibition of images had directed the Jews to a different vision of the divine.

For the most part, the Nabataeans remained true to their vision of rectangular anonymity for their gods. Their great god Dushara, their two chief goddesses Allat and al-'Uzza, as well as a cluster of lesser deities — all were represented as *betyls*. It was contact with the gods of the Greek, Roman and Egyptian worlds that modified their vision for, from the time of Alexander the Great on, many of these foreign deities, who had both names and human forms, became identified with Nabataean counterparts. Even this did not fundamentally alter the traditional concept as long as the Nabataean kingdom survived — a human representation portrays the assimilated foreign god rather than the original Nabataean deity. Only after the Roman annexation of Nabataea do we find anthropomorphic images of Nabataean gods. Until then, the closest the Nabataeans came to representing their gods in their own image was to adorn a small handful of their rectangular *betyls* with schematized facial features — a straight bar for the nose; eyes that are square, or in the shape of a four-pointed star, or oval; and, more rarely, an oval mouth.

Sometimes the distinction between foreign and local gods is subtle; but a double relief carving in Wadi Farasa in Petra shows an unblurred differentiation in iconography — above a simple *betyl* is a human head inside a circular medallion. It is as if the mason wished to clarify the identity of the unadorned block by carving vine leaves round the head above — a symbol of Dionysus who was commonly identified with Dushara. It indicates that abstract representations of Nabataean deities existed side by side with anthropomorphic images of the assimilated gods; the one was not superseded by the other.

UNDER AN OVERHANGING
ROCK IN WADI FARASA IN
PETRA AN ABSTRACT,
RECTANGULAR
REPRESENTATION OF THE
GREAT GOD DUSHARA HAS
ABOVE IT A HUMAN IMAGE OF
THE GREEK GOD DIONYSUS,
ONE OF MANY DEITIES WITH
WHOM DUSHARA WAS
IDENTIFIED.

such he was also associated with Dushara in Petra, where the cult of Isis was already well established. A handsome carved sandstone head, with abundant curls and full beard, found in Petra in 1958, has been identified as Zeus-Serapis; to which pairing, by extension, we may add Dushara.

As the last two Nabataean kings, Malichus II and Rabbel II, increasingly resided at Bostra, so Dushara acquired an association with the local Syrian god, who appears in an inscription at Hegra as 'A'ra who is at Bostra'. All the known references to Dushara-A'ra come from the Hauran, either in Bostra itself or nearby, and the dual cult outlived Rabbel's kingdom into the era of the Roman province of Arabia. At Umm al-Jimal in the southern Hauran an undated, but certainly Roman-period, stele was put up by 'Masheko, son of Awida, in honour of Dushara-A'ra'; and in Bostra itself a stele was 'dedicated by Yamlik, son of Masheko, for his own health and the health of his children, in honour of Dushara-A'ra, in… year 42 of the province' (AD 148). If these two Mashekos are the same person, we have a touching example of family loyalty to the local and national god over two generations.

To judge from the Roman-period coins of Bostra the cult of A'ra seems to have lost ground for Dushara alone is represented. There is also a striking ambivalence over portraying Dushara as a *betyl* or in human form — yet even the latter is in Arab, rather than Roman, guise. An AD 177 coin shows a handsome young profile, a wreath around his head, with the legend *Bostrenon Dusares* (Dushara of the Bostrans). The image shows both Roman and Nabataean influence — the god looks like a cross between Dionysus and a coin portrait of a Nabataean king. An almost identical depiction of the god appears on a coin of AD 244, in the reign of the Emperor Philip, the first Arab to occupy the imperial throne of Rome. But other coins portray Dushara as a traditional *betyl*, with a smaller one on either side. Though unnamed, one of these subordinate *betyls* is thought to represent the now evidently demoted A'ra.[4]

The greatest accolade to Dushara's status under Roman rule is seen in the Greek-style games that were organized in Bostra under Philip the Arab to celebrate the 1000th anniversary of the founding of Rome. Coins struck to commemorate this significant event call it Actia Dusaria – linking Augustus' victory at Actium in 31 BC with the great Nabataean god. Dushara had survived all foreign assimilations to be honoured in his Arabian name, in a Greek manner, in the heart of the Roman provinces, in the reign of an Arabian Roman emperor.

Two other Arabian gods — also known by epithets rather than names — figure in the lives and worship of the Nabataeans. Shay' al-Qaum, 'he who accompanies the people', is seen as the protector of the clan, travelling with the trading caravans and overseeing their welfare. He was the only truly nomadic god in the Nabataean pantheon, with no known portfolio that might relate to settled agricultural societies. He is referred to in inscriptions in Hegra and in the Hauran during the Nabataean period; but there is no mention of him at all in Petra, in whose increasingly luxurious lifestyle his ascetic qualities would doubtless have been out of place. For he remained sternly non-alcoholic and this, together with his tough, belligerent character, made him an ideal guardian for both nomads and soldiers. An inscription in Palmyra — a dedication in AD 132 of two altars by 'Ubaid son of Ghanim, who specifically identifies himself as both a Nabataean and a cavalryman — invokes 'Shay' al-Qaum, the good and bountiful god, who never drinks wine'. While settled elements of Nabataean society no longer shrank from wine, it was clearly as inappropriate an indulgence for armies as it was for caravans on their long journeys through arid deserts. Shay' al-Qaum, it seems, never adapted to a settled life, an indication that many Nabataeans remained in some sense nomadic, being either soldiers or involved in the long-distance caravan trade.

More references are known to the god al-Kutba, 'the great scribe', than to Shay' al-Qaum. Curiously, al-Kutba is described as 'an Arab goddess' in Syriac literature from Edessa in the third to eighth centuries; but there is no concrete evidence for femininity in inscriptions within the Nabataean kingdom — indeed, an inscription in Petra refers to 'al-Kutba, this very god' in a specifically masculine form. As his name implies (from the Arabic *ktb* – write), he was the scribe of the gods and the patron of writing, divination and commerce. He had an impressive range of identifications, including the Arabian Ruda and Graeco-Roman Hermes-Mercury. The latter assimilation may also have endowed him with the role of messenger of the gods, interpreter of the divine will, guide of travellers (an overlap with Shay' al-Qaum), protector of shepherds and accompanier of the spirits of the dead to the underworld.

UMM AL-JIMAL IN THE HAURAN REGION IN THE NORTH OF THE NABATAEAN KINGDOM, WHERE THE COMPOSITE GOD DUSHARA-A'RA WAS FREQUENTLY MENTIONED IN INSCRIPTIONS. AN IMPORTANT STOP ON A CARAVAN ROUTE, UMM AL-JIMAL WAS DEVELOPED BY THE NABATAEANS BEFORE BEING REBUILT BY THE ROMANS AND EXTENDED DURING THE BYZANTINE ERA.

Two temples dedicated to al-Kutba are known outside the Nabataean kingdom. At Tell ash-Shuqafiya in the eastern Egyptian Delta, around the time that Wahb'allahi made his 'quadrangular shrine' there to Dushara in the late first century BC, a devotee built a temple 'for al-Kutba the god, for the life of our lord Seyo, the priest, and for his own life and in order that his name be remembered'. In the same century, at a caravan station in northern Sinai now called Qasr-awet, one of two Nabataean temples there was also dedicated to al-Kutba.

An intriguing reference to the god is found in the open rock sanctuary of 'Ain Shellaleh in Wadi Rum. Two niches, with

a *betyl* relief in each, are carved side by side and beneath them an inscription identifies that on the left as the goddess al-'Uzza, while on the right is 'al-Kutba who is in Gaia'. Both have schematic 'star' eyes and a raised band for a nose, though al-Kutba's features are badly damaged. The association of al-'Uzza with al-Kutba; the statement that al-Kutba 'is in Gaia', home of Dushara; and the likely identification of both al-Kutba and Dushara with Ruda – all this points to the possibility that these two apparently distinct Nabataean gods, Dushara and al-Kutba, with their epithet-names, may represent two different aspects of Ruda. And, if other scholars are correct,[5] Shay' al-Qaum may have been another aspect of the same divinity – the third member of a kind of Nabataean trinity.

The three Arabian sister-goddesses, Allat, al-'Uzza and Manat, form another trinity. The 'Alilat' mentioned by Herodotus – or al-Ilat, the feminine form of al-Ilah (god) – is clearly Allat, the principal goddess of northern Arabia. Herodotus identifies her with Aphrodite, but more common identifications were with Athena, the Greek goddess of war, and with the Syrian earth goddess, Atargatis. Outside the Nabataean kingdom she is mentioned in Lihyanite texts from the Hellenistic period at Dedan, just south of Hegra; the tribe of Thamud also worshipped her; she was the deity most frequently invoked in Safaitic inscriptions; and at Palmyra a fine temple was dedicated to her.

Within Nabataea one of the most important centres of Allat's worship was Wadi Rum, and inscriptions all over the vast Rum wadi system refer to her. The temple of Rum, built in the reign of Rabbel II though on an earlier foundation, was dedicated to 'Allat, the goddess who is at Iram' (the ancient name for Rum); and inside it the excavators found both a rectangular *betyl* and a fragment of a statue of a goddess – perhaps the original image and its Roman-period replacement, for Allat-Athena remained popular in the province of Arabia. But if Rabbel II developed the cult of Allat in Iram, he did not initiate it, for the goddess was already venerated in the rock sanctuary of 'Ain Shellaleh, a short distance from the temple. An inscription beside the spring – a prayer inscribed in stone – was dedicated to her by masons (probably working on the new temple) who asked to be remembered 'for good and for blessing'. There is also

WADI SIYYAGH, RUNNING WEST OUT OF PETRA, CONTAINS ONE OF THE CITY'S MOST ABUNDANT SPRINGS. THE SANCTITY
OF WATER FOR THE NABATAEANS CAN BE SEEN IN THE NUMBER OF SACRED NICHES CARVED INTO THE CLIFFS ABOVE THE
STREAM; ONE OF THESE IS DEDICATED TO ATARGATIS, THE SYRIAN GODDESS OF FERTILITY, VEGETATION AND WATER.

form, are found in and around Palmyra, but within the Nabataean kingdom the place where she is most often mentioned is Hegra. This may be because at Petra so few tomb inscriptions have survived, and Manat's role is particularly appropriate to the legalities of tomb ownership and rights of burial — in which Hegra has unrivalled documentation in the Nabataean world. In eight out of the multitude of Hegra tomb inscriptions we find Manat (twice with an associate deity — 'her Qaysha') linked with Dushara in cursing those who might in the future violate the terms of use for the tomb:

> This is the tomb which 'Aydu son of Kuhaylu son of Alkasi made for himself and his children and his descendants and for whoever produces in his hand a deed of entitlement from the hand of 'Aydu... And may Dushara and Manat and her Qaysha curse anyone who sells this tomb or buys it or gives it in pledge or makes a gift of it or leases it.

In other tomb inscriptions Manat is also involved in the fine to be imposed for non-observance of the specified rules, and which presumably was to go to the temple: 'And whoever does other than what is above will be liable to a fine to Dushara and Manat in the sum of 1000 Haretite selas, and to our lord Rabbel, king of the Nabataeans, for the same amount.'

Although there is no direct portrayal of Manat at Hegra, there is what appears to be an indirect representation. One tomb façade (whose brief inscription makes no mention of the goddess) has a relief carving of two griffins facing each other, and between them a rosette inscribed in a circle — a stylized image of the wheel of fate of Nemesis-Manat.[7]

When the Nabataeans settled in Edom and Syria, they adopted some of the local deities who already presided over these lands, while still retaining their distinct characters. Atargatis — the 'Syrian goddess' who presided over vegetation, fertility and water — had her main sanctuary at Manbij (the Hierapolis of the Romans) in northern Syria, where she was worshipped together with Hadad, the Syrian god of heaven, rain and fertility. According to Diodorus, in a fit of jealousy Aphrodite had made the divine Atargatis fall in love with a Syrian mortal named Caystrus, by whom she became pregnant. In shame Atargatis threw herself into the water, whereupon she became half fish. Having killed Caystrus, she then exposed her daughter in the mountains, but the baby was saved by some doves who stole milk and cheese from the local shepherds to feed her. Eventually the shepherds found her and brought her to their chief who named

A TOMB FAÇADE IN HEGRA (TODAY'S MEDA'IN SALEH IN NORTH-WEST SAUDI ARABIA) WITH A RELIEF CARVING OF TWO GRIFFINS FACING EACH OTHER ACROSS A ROSETTE INSCRIBED IN A CIRCLE — A STYLIZED IMAGE OF THE WHEEL OF FATE OF THE GODDESS MANAT.

her Semiramis — 'the one who comes from the doves'. Strange religious practices were associated with the cult of Atargatis, including the voluntary castration of her devotees.

In Petra there is a *betyl* with square eyes whose inscription names her as 'Atargatis of Manbij' — a curious assimilation into Nabataean style, for the Syrian goddess was usually represented in human form. As if to underline Atargatis' role as the goddess of vegetation and springs, the *betyl* is carved on a rock not far from the main spring of Petra in Wadi Siyyagh.

Besides Hadad, whose worship was associated with that of Atargatis, two other deities appear to have been adopted. Qos, a shadowy god apparently worshipped by the Edomites, had links with Hadad, god of storms and rain; both seem to have had the same functions of agricultural growth and fecundity, and shared the same attributes – bulls, thunderbolts and eagles. Both may have been identified with Dushara, though there is no direct evidence for this; but they were certainly identified with the great Canaanite-Phoenician god, Ba'al-Shamin, whose cult had spread into Syria and as far as Mesopotamia by the first century BC.

Ba'al-Shamin, whose name means 'lord of heaven', was also lord of the earth and god of vegetation. Though he shared the same attributes as Qos and Hadad, he was especially represented by an eagle with outstretched wings, and by ears of wheat and a cornucopia with grapes. He does not appear to have been identified with Dushara; indeed an inscription at 'Ain Shellaleh in Wadi Rum, to 'Dushara and Ba'al-Shamin, gods of our lord' (Rabbel II), indicates that in Nabataean eyes they were distinct. Wadi Rum was not the only place in the Nabataean heartland where this foreign god was invoked – an early-first-century AD inscription was found near the remains of a Nabataean temple in Wadi Mousa (ancient Gaia): 'This is the sanctuary built for Ba'al-Shamin, the god of Malichus.' He may even have been worshipped in the heart of Petra for an inscription found in Qasr al-Bint to 'Zeus *hypsistos*' (most high) uses the particular epithet of Zeus, with which Ba'al-Shamin was more usually identified than Dushara. But his main home was in the Hauran.

At Si'a in the Hauran, about 30 km north-east of Bostra, lies a remote ancient sanctuary, unassociated with any settlement. Its position is serenely beautiful, set on the end of a low ridge overlooking vast stretches of the rolling, fertile plains that surround the volcanic cone of Jabal al-Arab. For long it was thought of as Nabataean because of some features of its buildings – mainly the plain, horned capitals; also the script in which many of its inscriptions had been carved (others are in Greek, or bilingual), some Nabataean personal names in the inscriptions and, supremely, the supposed dedication of one temple to Dushara. In fact, except for the short period when Aretas III extended his rule as far as Damascus, Si'a lay outside the Nabataean kingdom; but its proximity to Bostra and the Nabataean territory immediately to the south inevitably meant that it was greatly influenced by Nabataean style.

A RECONSTRUCTION OF THE FAÇADE OF THE TEMPLE OF BA'AL-SHAMIN AT SI'A. FOUR STATUES STOOD IN THE PORTICO, INCLUDING ONE OF HEROD THE GREAT. FROM H. C. BUTLER'S *ANCIENT ARCHITECTURE IN SYRIA*, SECTION A, PART 6, 1916.

THE CONICAL HILL IN WADI HASA ON
WHICH STANDS KHIRBET AT-TANNUR,
ONCE A GREAT NABATAEAN TEMPLE AND
CENTRE OF PILGRIMAGE. EXCAVATED IN
1937 BY A JOINT JORDANIAN-AMERICAN
TEAM, THE WEALTH OF SCULPTURE
FOUND THERE IS NOW DIVIDED
BETWEEN CINCINNATI ART MUSEUM IN
THE UNITED STATES, AND THE
ARCHAEOLOGICAL MUSEUM IN AMMAN,
JORDAN.

as burnt offerings to the gods 2000 years before. Though built within a Nabataean cultural context, this tower-altar has more in common with the Syrian-Phoenician tradition than with the Nabataean.

Then, probably at the end of the first century AD or early in the second — just at the time that the new temple complex was being built at Khirbet adh-Dharih — the sanctuary on Jabal at-Tannur was expanded to occupy the entire mountain-top. A great stone-paved temenos was created, with four triclinia around its outer edge for the ritual feasts that were a part of the cult. At its centre was the earlier altar which was now enclosed in a 2-metre-square building, with an arched entrance on the east side, finely decorated with carved thunderbolts and foliate designs. Inside, against the original altar wall, were seated figures of the two deities to whom the temple was dedicated — the Edomite god, Qos, flanked by a bull and an eagle and carrying a thunderbolt, all identifying him with both Syrian Hadad and

The Syrian goddess, Atargatis, with dolphins over her head indicating her role as goddess of water. Found at Khirbet at-Tannur. (Amman Archaeological Museum)

The Edomite god Qos, identified with the Syrian Hadad, was the deity to whom the Nabataean sanctuary at Khirbet at-Tannur was dedicated — perhaps by descendants of the Edomites who continued to live in the Nabataean kingdom and became an integrated element in the population. (Amman Archaeological Museum)

Ba'al-Shamin; and beside him Atargatis, the Syrian goddess of vegetation, fertility and fish. A larger and more spectacular representation of Atargatis — a bust, surrounded by flowers and with face and neck covered with leaves — crowned the entrance, and over her head stood an eagle with outspread wings, an attribute of Qos, Hadad and Ba'al-Shamin.

The identity of the god is known not just from the clear iconography, but also from a fragment of an inscription on an altar: 'which Qosmilik made for Qos, the god of Harawa'. It is thought that Harawa, which means 'burned', might refer to the strikingly black volcanic outcrop in Wadi Hasa, very near Jabal at-Tannur. No inscription mentions Atargatis, who is known from her imagery alone: the lions that are one of her main attributes; ears of wheat, fruit, flowers and leaves, all connected with her role as goddess of vegetation; snakes; and the dolphins which recall her fishy associations. But to judge from the two seated figures inside the central shrine, the prominent bust of the goddess over the entrance, with the eagle on her head, and from the extraordinary number of representations of her, it seems very likely that the sanctuary was dedicated to Atargatis as well as to Qos.

In the second century the temple had yet another, and considerably larger, structure built around it, decorated on either side by several busts of Atargatis, each with a different attribute underlining her varying roles. Particularly striking, and well preserved, are those portraying her as grain goddess and dolphin

goddess. With its wealth of sculpture, the sanctuary of Khirbet at-Tannur may well have been the most richly decorated pilgrimage centre in the Nabataean kingdom; and the huge number of small dedicatory altars, and also of terracotta votive offerings, suggests that it may also have been the most frequented – probably, like Khirbet adh-Dharih, for celebrations of the main festivals in the Nabataean calendar. Evidence for this can be seen in the carving of the zodiac surrounding a bust of Tyche (Fortune), borne by a winged Nike; the signs of the zodiac are not in their normal order, but are divided into two groups of six, corresponding to the spring and autumn seasons with their strong agricultural connotations. The sanctuary appears to have continued to function until the late third or mid-fourth century AD.

The sculptures of both Khirbet at-Tannur and Khirbet adh-Dharih are so similar that it is thought they must come from the same teams of artists, and to judge from their style they were members of a local workshop. In particular, the winged Nike figures, found in some profusion in both sites, are like peas out of the same pod. That the craftsmen actually worked on site, and not in some remote studio, is evident from the few unfinished busts that were found at Khirbet at-Tannur. The frontal angle, symmetrical facial features, prominent eyes, thick lips and stylized curly hairstyle of these figures have more in common with the rustic oriental tradition of Syria, albeit overlaid with Hellenistic influence, than with Nabataean art as seen in Petra. This distinct style, and the representations of Edomite and Syrian gods, suggest that this 'Nabataean' site may in fact have been the work of descendants of the Edomites, who pursued their lives, worshipping their own gods, throughout the period of the Nabataean kingdom and into the Roman provincial era.

A WINGED VICTORY (NIKE) FROM KHIRBET AT-TANNUR, CARRYING ON HER HEAD A BUST OF TYCHE SURROUNDED BY A ZODIAC DISC. THE SIGNS, INSTEAD OF FOLLOWING THE NORMAL ORDER, ARE DIVIDED INTO TWO GROUPS OF SIX, THOSE REPRESENTING THE SPRING CALENDAR ON THE LEFT AND THOSE OF AUTUMN ON THE RIGHT. THE WINGED NIKE, WITH THE LOWER PART OF THE ZODIAC DISC, IS IN AMMAN ARCHAEOLOGICAL MUSEUM. THE ROUNDEL WITH THE TYCHE AND MOST OF THE DISC IS IN CINCINNATI ART MUSEUM.

SEVEN

LANGUAGE, SCRIPT AND GRAFFITI

Speaking Arabic, Writing Aramaic
and Carving Inscriptions

Above ONE OF THE LARGEST TOMBS AT HEGRA, WITH A ROW OF CAPITALS BETWEEN THE CORNICES AND A CARVING OF A SPHINX ON THE LOWER CORNERS OF THE PEDIMENT ABOVE THE ENTRANCE.

Left A HEGRA TOMB, WITH EAGLE AND URNS OVER THE MAIN ENTRANCE.

Below THE EVENING SUN FALLS ON A ROW OF TOMB FAÇADES CARVED INTO ONE SIDE OF A ROCK OUTCROP CALLED QASR AL-BINT IN THE HEART OF HEGRA.

Right One of the smaller and simpler tomb façades at Hegra.

Below A Nabataean plain capital at Hegra.

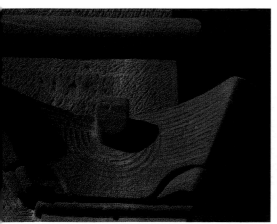

decoration, with not a broken pediment or tholos to be seen. Petra pediments (apart from the Khazneh) do not have eagles with swept-back wings, or (with a few exceptions) urns; these are more or less standard in Hegra. Nor do we often find Petra tombs adorned with near-human faces, like tragic masks, with snakes radiating out like Medusa locks; nor are there sphinxes or griffins, nor many rosettes and solar discs. All these are commonly found here. But the chief glory of Hegra is the wealth of inscriptions which give an insight not only into the people who lived here, their names, lives, relationships and occupations, but also into their laws and their gods, the position of women and rights of ownership.

Of the 80 or so tomb façades in Hegra, 37 have inscriptions (some more than one), and 33 of these include a date, of which 28 fall between I BC and AD 74 – an unrivalled collection of Nabataean texts from a clearly defined time-span. Though the Turkmaniyya tomb in Petra also falls within this period, the sophistication of its calligraphy and the careful planning to arrange the text well in the available space are nowhere matched in Hegra. The Turkmaniyya inscription is a fluent example of

A PEDIMENT ABOVE THE ENTRANCE PORTAL TO A HEGRA TOMB, WITH AN EAGLE AND TWO URNS AT THE CORNERS, AND INSIDE A MASK-LIKE FACE WITH SNAKES RADIATING OUT LIKE MEDUSA LOCKS.

the workmanship of a metropolitan atelier; at Hegra we see the output of provincial stone cutters with varying levels of expertise. It is thought that the men who cut the inscriptions would have copied onto stone the text that professional scribes had written on papyrus. Some achieved fine calligraphy and laid the text out well; others appear ill at ease with letters, carving them in a disorganized manner. They may have been illiterate. In some cases the workman ran out of space inside the area that had been specially prepared for the inscription, perhaps because of his own inept planning, or maybe because the client tiresomely extended the text in the middle of the job. The solutions were basic, practical and untroubled by aesthetics: the stone cutter might cramp some characters into too small a space; or simply continue carving the supernumerary words on the rougher surface below the prepared area; or, if there was a raised border

THE INTERIOR OF A HEGRA TOMB, SHOWING BURIAL SLOTS CUT INTO THE WALL. SOME OF THE INSCRIPTIONS SPECIFY WHICH MEMBERS OF THE FAMILY MIGHT BE BURIED IN EACH SIDE OF THE TOMB.

not only indicates something of the later history of this southern outpost, but also provides a fascinating preview of what was to become of the Nabataean language and script. It records the burial of Raqush, daughter of 'Abdmanutu of the tribe of Thamud, in AD 267/8, 160 years after the Romans had taken over the Nabataean kingdom. That Roman rule extended to the Hejaz as well as to all other parts of the erstwhile Nabataean kingdom is evident from another inscription, bilingual Nabataean-Greek, on a temple built at Ruwwafa, some 125 km northwest of Hegra, by a confederation of the Thamud. It was dedicated by them to the Emperor Marcus Aurelius, and to Lucius Verus, his brother and co-emperor from AD 161 to 169. The inscription also mentions two Roman governors of the province of Arabia, one of whom may have acted as peacemaker between factions of the Thamud. Evidence for Roman military presence was found just south of Hegra in Greek graffiti engraved on the rocks by soldiers of the *ala Gaetulorum* and the *ala dromedariorum* (camel corps); and in Hegra itself a stele was found commemorating a painter whose job was to decorate shields for the 3rd Cyrenaica legion that was stationed in the area.

These inscriptions show that, just as the Nabataeans had usurped Hegra from the Lihyanites, so, some time after the Roman annexation, a confederation of the tribe of Thamud began to dominate this area of the Hejaz, possibly integrating peacefully with the Nabataean population. Nabataean culture clearly remained strong – the Ruwwafa inscription indicates that the Thamudic people adopted the language and script used by the Nabataeans, at least for formal inscriptions. Yet the Thamudic script still appears a century after this on the bilingual tomb inscription from Hegra – perhaps as a deliberate message that Thamudic culture had not disappeared without trace.

On closer study, scholars found that the Nabataean part of the Raqush tomb inscription was not quite what it seemed, for though the script is certainly Nabataean, the language is more related to Arabic than to Aramaic. The evolution of a script for the as yet unwritten Arabic language, using Nabataean characters, may have begun some time before; but by the second half of the third century AD, when this inscription was carved in Hegra – and also a large number of those in the Sinai – the process was well under way.

Nabataean occupation of the Sinai peninsula had probably begun in the third century BC, at about the same time that other Nabataean groups were settling in Edom and the Hauran, and taking control of the Hegra area. Traders and herders, they used

WHEN THE NABATAEANS CAME INTO THE SINAI PENINSULA, PROBABLY IN THE SECOND CENTURY BC, THEY USED THE EXISTING ANCIENT ROUTES THROUGH THE MOUNTAINS AND WADIS. HERE, AMID THE GRANITE FORMATIONS AROUND MOUNT SINAI, AS ELSEWHERE IN THE PENINSULA, THEY MOVED THEIR FLOCKS OR TRADING CARAVANS.

the ancient routes established since time immemorial by the nomadic tribes that peopled the Sinai, passing along wadis, between mountains that presented an ever-changing panorama of geological formations. There are wildly eroded sandstone mountains, varying in colour from the oldest red Cambrian, about 600 million years old, through pale-grey Ordovician, to whitish Silurian, each gradation of colour separated by about 100 million years. The sandstone gives way to soaring mountains of red

pre-Cambrian granite at the heart of southern Sinai, around which is a ring of black volcanic rhyolite peaks, a mere ten million years old. Harshest of all are the iron-rich sandstone hills in the north, oxidized over the millennia to a sombre black, with sand drifting up their jagged slopes. Here and there in southern Sinai, on low rises overlooking these routes, the Nabataeans would have seen – as the modern visitor still does – homely clusters of circular tombs, their entrances facing the setting sun. Those Nabataeans of 2000 years ago could not have known that these tombs were then already over 3000 years old.

Over the following centuries some groups gave up their wanderings to settle in places, like Wadi Feiran, where a regular water supply and agriculture made sedentary life possible.

A CLUSTER OF FOURTH MILLENNIUM BC TOMBS NEAR ONE OF THE NABATAEAN ROUTES THROUGH THE SINAI PENINSULA. WHEN THE NABATAEANS SAW THEM THESE TOMBS WERE ALREADY 3000 YEARS OLD.

Several of these Nabataean-related groups became known by the places in which they settled, and a few are named by ancient authors: Pharanites (from Pharan/Wadi Feiran), Garindeans (from Gharandal near Suez), Raitheni (from Raithu, today's at-Tur) and Autaei (from Qasr-awet in the north). Other groups continued their itinerant lives, making their way along steep-sided wadis, in some places broad and sandy, in others closing to a narrow defile. At the point of narrowing, the underlying water was squeezed nearer the surface, forming oases where palms and tamarisk and other plants flourished, and where water for drinking could be reached easily. Here the herders could water their flocks, and the traders could do business with the people who had settled in the area.

In many wadis – especially Mukatteb in the west, Haggag in the east and Feiran in the centre – as they sheltered from the sun in the heat of the day, these tribesmen carved on the rocks their names and messages of peace and good wishes, as well as pictures of the camels, horses, donkeys and ibex that were part of their lives. Just as Niebuhr had supposed, most of these

WADI FEIRAN, ONE OF MOST ABUNDANTLY WATERED PLACES IN SINAI. HERE MANY PEOPLE, INCLUDING NABATAEANS, GAVE UP THEIR WANDERINGS FOR A SETTLED AGRICULTURAL WAY OF LIFE GROWING DATES. OF THOSE WHO REMAINED NOMADIC, HERDSMEN WOULD STOP HERE FOR WATER AND PASTURE, AND TRADERS TO DO BUSINESS.

'Sinaitic Inscriptions', which had caused such a stir in the eighteenth and nineteenth centuries, consisted of little more than names, 'executed at idle hours by travellers... but little skilled in the arts'; Burckhardt was also right in suggesting that 'they consist merely of short phrases, all similar to each other'. Beer had confirmed these suppositions, based as they were on careful first-hand observation; he had correctly ascribed the inscriptions to the Nabataeans (or a related tribe) and, while he identified the language as Aramaic, he also noticed the inclusion of Arabic forms, words and names; and he had provided accurate translations, including the most common initial greetings – 'Peace! Taimu son of Garmalba'ali'; 'Remember Zaidu, Aushu, Harishu and Sha'du'; 'Bless Waddu son of Noshaigu.'

SOME OF THE NABATAEAN INSCRIPTIONS, WRITTEN ON FLAT STONES WHICH
FORM PART OF THE BUILDING MATERIAL OF THE ENCLOSURE ON TOP OF JABAL
MUNEIJAH. THE INSCRIPTIONS REFER TO PRIESTS AND OTHER FOLLOWERS OF
SEVERAL GODS – BUT NO SPECIFICALLY NABATAEAN DEITIES ARE MENTIONED.

pastoralists and traders who rested for a while at the oasis before
continuing on their way. When the connection with Moses was
made is unknown, but for many centuries, and up to very recent
times, the bedouin of the area performed a pilgrimage at least
once a year, and maybe more frequently, to the top of Jabal
Muneijah. It was particularly honoured by pastoralists who went
there to offer sacrifices to Moses, the great shepherd of the
Sinai, and to pray for the prosperity of their flocks and herds.
Some time after the advent of Islam the pilgrimage became associated with the Eid al-Adha, the greatest of the Islamic feasts,
when sheep are slaughtered to celebrate the averted sacrifice of
Ishmael.[12] Yet the pilgrimage appears to have originated in the
Nabataean period, when sacrifices to the gods were offered at the
high place on the summit of Jabal Muneijah.

By the fourth century AD, Nabataean inscriptions were no
longer being carved in the Sinai – nor were they common any-
where else. After at least 700 years of speaking Arabic and writing Aramaic, the strain between the two languages was clearly
beginning to tell. As early as around AD 100, the Oboda inscription appears to contain Arabic poetry in the Nabataean script
(see pages 47–48); Beer had noticed Arabisms in the Sinai
inscriptions of the second and third centuries AD; and the
Raqush tomb inscription (AD 267/8) from Hegra has been
shown to be more Arabic than Aramaic in its language, though
still written in the Nabataean script. By AD 328 another burial
inscription, found at Namara in the Hauran, has taken the transition a step further for, while the script is an elegant and (for a
stone carving) fairly cursive Nabataean, the language is almost
completely Arabic. But linguistic Luddites were at large, resisting
the trend towards using the script they wrote in to express the
language they spoke: in AD 356, also in Hegra, an inscription
was carved in both the Nabataean Aramaic script and language.

The few surviving examples of handwriting in ink on
papyrus, seen at its best in some of the Babatha documents,

show that outside the world of stone-carving a more cursive form of the Nabataean script was commonly used, with most letters joined to those before and after. How the final stages of the transition were made – from Arabic-in-the-Nabataean-script to Arabic-in-the-Arabic-script – is unclear. There are no known Nabataean inscriptions from the fifth century; but there are three short carved texts from the sixth century,[13] in varying styles of proto-Arabic, that both look backward to the late Nabataean cursive forms and forward to the Arabic script of the earliest period of Islam in the seventh century, which was developed into an artform of surpassing beauty as the script of the Koran.

Beer had already noticed that different letters in the Nabataean Aramaic alphabet were written almost identically; hence it was difficult to differentiate between 'b' and 'n', 'r' and 'z', 'p' (which in Arabic later became 'f') and 'q', and several other pairs of letters, except by the context. This required considerable fluency in the written language. To ease this problem for readers, the Arabic scribes introduced diacritical marks onto the basic Aramaic characters to clarify their sound value and comprehend the greater number of consonants in Arabic.

The Nabataeans, caught up as they were in the Roman Empire which in the fourth century dissolved into the Greek-speaking Christian Byzantine Empire, followed the trend of their rulers and neighbours. Greek had now become the lingua franca of the Middle East; and all the people of the region, while speaking and writing their own languages for everyday purposes, used Greek for virtually all official documents. But Arabic, the spoken and increasingly written native language of the Nabataeans, survived long after Greek had disappeared from the Middle East.

EIGHT

BABATHA

The Life, Loves and Litigation of a
Woman among the Nabataeans

THE VIEW THAT BABATHA WOULD HAVE HAD IN THE LAST MONTHS OF HER LIFE. LOOKING SOUTH-EAST OVER NAHAL HEVER TOWARDS THE DEAD SEA, SHE COULD HAVE WATCHED GRIFFON VULTURES PLANING UP AND DOWN THE VALLEY, WHILE ON THE PLATEAU ABOUT 60 METRES ABOVE HER HEAD THE ROMANS HAD BUILT A CAMP, AND WAITED…

O N 19 AUGUST AD 132 a young widow living at Mahoza on the south-eastern shore of the Dead Sea, in the erstwhile Nabataean kingdom, went to the village registry to receive three months' maintenance money for her son from one of his official guardians. Young as she was — probably still in her twenties — she had already been twice widowed. Her son was from her first marriage; she had no children by her second husband — at least, none that had survived. In the torrid summer heat of the rift valley she waited while a receipt was written for the guardian, complete with a subscript and signature on her behalf by her legal representative; then another was written for the young woman herself, word for word. Babatha always kept a copy, even though she could not read or write, for she knew from bitter experience the value of written, certified evidence of any transaction regarding money or property.

The scribe, Germanos son of Judah, knew Babatha well; he had written several legal documents, plus copies, for this fellow-Jew and for other members of her family, each time struggling with his rather patchy command of Greek. Most had been summonses to court or depositions, either by Babatha against some of her relatives by marriage or by those same relatives against Babatha — Germanos knew a great deal about her acrimonious family disputes. This latest visit must have seemed to the scribe sadly lacking its customary drama.

Germanos rolled up the papyrus scroll, bound it with string and had the witnesses sign in the prescribed places. Then he gave it to Babatha, who put it carefully inside her leather pouch together with a group of other scrolls, all of which related to her young son Jesus and her disputes with his guardians. Three times she had sought a ruling on Roman guardianship law, and these documents were also filed away in her pouch. Other scrolls were neatly bundled together by subject — there were bills of sale of the plots of land she owned in and around Mahoza, and the official declaration of all her property, made in the Roman census less than five years before; there was the marriage contract to her second husband, Judah son of Eleazar Khthusion, with all its clear statements of her rights and entitlements in the event of his death; then, after Judah's death, there were long-drawn-out property disputes with his first wife; and others with the guardians of the orphans of Judah's brother. Every scrap of official writing that might be needed as evidence of her legal rights was stored away in case any of these disputes should rear its head again.

Now whatever unfinished business there might have been had to be put on hold. Babatha and the other Jewish residents of Mahoza felt profoundly insecure. In the province of Judaea to the west, Simon Bar Kokhba had recently launched the second Jewish revolt against Roman rule and was doing brilliantly well — by August 132 he had adopted the title Premier of Israel and had taken possession of the Emperor Hadrian's land at Ein Gedi on the western shore of the Dead Sea. In the province of Arabia, although there is little direct evidence of disturbance, the indirect evidence suggests that the Roman governor, Haterius Nepos, was mobilizing all the forces he could muster to help crush the revolt in Judaea, which was proving far more successful than the Romans had at first expected.[1] Although the Jews in Arabia enjoyed excellent relations with their Nabataean neighbours, they must now have felt vulnerable to possible reprisals by the Romans who would have seen them, if not as active collaborators, then at least as passive supporters of Bar Kokhba's attempted coup d'état. The Jews doubtless concluded that at Ein Gedi, now firmly in rebel hands, they would surely be safer.

We can only guess at the line of arguments that resulted in Babatha's flight to Bar Kokhba's would-be Jewish state. Her second husband had been born in Ein Gedi, as had many other Jewish residents of Mahoza, and it seems logical that they went there first. But then Hadrian sent his best generals against the rebels – in particular Julius Severus, who had been hurriedly extracted from his prestigious governorship of Britain to meet the extreme emergency in Judaea. Then, as the Romans closed in on Ein Gedi, the inhabitants fled into the surrounding hills, taking with them as much as they could carry of their most treasured possessions. Babatha, together with her son and a number of their neighbours from Mahoza, apparently went with a group of leading Bar Kokhba supporters to a large complex of caves in the precipitous slopes of Nahal Hever, a valley a short distance south of Ein Gedi. When the Romans discovered their hiding place and set up camp on the plateau above, the occupants hid their belongings, including letters from Bar Kokhba himself, in some of the cracks and crevices in the cave walls. Babatha put her precious leather pouch, wrapped in sacking, tied with rope and tucked inside a water-skin, into a crevice in a corner of the cave; over it she (or a fellow refugee) placed a wicker basket containing a painted jewellery box, four wooden dishes, a pair of sandals, some keys, knives and a sickle.

ROMAN SOLDIERS IN BATTLE, FROM THE ARCH OF GALERIUS, SALONIKA (PHOTO: F.H.C. BIRCH, SONIA HALLIDAY PHOTOGRAPHS).

Other skins containing personal belongings were also crammed in, and stones were pushed into the mouth of the crevice, effectively concealing their hiding place.

Over 1800 years later, in March 1961,[2] a team of archaeologists excavating in this cave in Nahal Hever, in search of materials from the Bar Kokhba period, found not only Bar Kokhba's letters but also several caches of documents, clothes and household goods which, though mostly perished or eaten by moths and worms, were of high quality. These were the possessions of wealthy people. Among them they found Babatha's collection of 35 papyrus documents – six in the Nabataean form of Aramaic, three in Jewish Aramaic, the remainder in Greek (though some have Nabataean and Aramaic signatures and subscripts). Together they provide the most comprehensive picture so far discovered of rural life and society, and of family and property law, in the period from the end of the Nabataean kingdom into the early years of the Roman province of Arabia.[3]

The documents show the easy relationship that existed between the Nabataean residents of Mahoza and the Jewish newcomers: property changed hands between them and water rights were carefully allocated, or shared, between neighbouring properties; Nabataeans acted as guardians for Jewish children, and both stood as witnesses and legal representatives for the others' law suits. They appear to have interacted in almost every way — perhaps even in marriage. This already had precedents: Herod the Great's mother was a Nabataean and one of his sons, Herod Antipas, had married (and divorced) a daughter of Aretas IV. Some names and patronymics in

avoid the gathering storm of the first Jewish revolt against the Romans (AD 66–74) by acquiring property on the fringes of the Nabataean kingdom. It was, after all, not far from his home town of Ein Gedi, particularly as the Dead Sea that lay between them was then used freely for transporting people and goods from place to place on either side. After the Romans' destruction of Jerusalem in AD 70, and their devastation of Ein Gedi, the trickle of émigrés became a flood. Many Jews fled to areas where they felt that the long arm of Roman retribution would not reach them; some moved to Nabataean territory despite the fact that King Malichus II, shortly before his death, had sent a large force to help the Romans in the siege of Jerusalem. Those Jews who could afford to do so bought land in productive areas such as Mahoza, where they could benefit from both the advanced Nabataean water technology and the well established and humane administration that covered both agricultural and social matters.

What is more difficult to conjecture is why the existing Nabataean owners wanted to sell their land. It could be that as both Malichus II and Rabbel II spent more time in Bostra, many Nabataeans chose to move to the rich agricultural lands that surrounded the main city in the north. The selling of their land here could also be an indication that some Nabataeans, many of whom had been settled farmers only since the time of Aretas IV, were responding to an urge to pull up their roots again and revert to their nomadic past.

Simon received for each plot of land a bill of sale written in the Nabataean script in the Nabataean registry in Mahoza. The date orchard he bought on 18 December AD 99 had belonged to a Nabataean woman called 'Abi'adan daughter of Aftah, to whom he paid the sum of 168 *sela'in*. Yet only one month previously 'Abi'adan had drawn up a virtually identical document for the sale of the same property to a certain Archelaus, the *strategos* – a Nabataean despite his Greek name – for only 112 *sela'in*. What had happened in the intervening month to produce an increase of 50 per cent on the sale price? We can only guess at the answer – perhaps Archelaus backed out of the deal; but what seems more likely, in view of the increased price, is that 'Abi'adan high-handedly rescinded her agreement with Archelaus when she received a better offer from Simon. Either way, it seems that these documents did not in themselves confer the final title to a property; there had to be a further stage in the process of transferring ownership – perhaps registering the property in the new owner's name 'with the public authorities',

'ON THE 3 OF KISLEV, IN THE 28TH YEAR OF RABBEL THE KING, … WHO BROUGHT LIFE AND DELIVERANCE TO HIS PEOPLE… AND IN THE LIFETIME OF OBODAS [HIS] SON… AND OF GAMILAT AND HAGERU HIS SISTERS, QUEENS OF THE NABATAEANS, CHILDREN OF MALICHUS [II]…' THIS 'DOUBLE' DOCUMENT OF 19 NOVEMBER AD 99 GIVES THE NAMES OF MEMBERS OF RABBEL II'S FAMILY (SEE PAGES 69 AND 73), AND THEN SPECIFIES THE PRICE (112 *SELA'IN*) FOR WHICH 'ABI'ADAN WILL SELL HER DATE ORCHARD TO ARCHELAUS, THE *STRATEGOS*, AND THE LEGAL AND WATER RIGHTS HE WILL RECEIVE. YET ONE MONTH LATER 'ABI'ADAN SOLD THE SAME PROPERTY TO BABATHA'S FATHER FOR 168 *SELA'IN*. (PHOTO: ISRAEL MUSEUM)

as specified in a later document. Both these documents relating to 'Abi'adan's date orchard passed into Simon's possession, and from him to Babatha.

Simon may have had some problems with deciphering the Nabataean script but the spoken language was at least comprehensible to someone familiar with the Jewish form of Aramaic. The legal terminology would have posed no difficulties since both Jews and Nabataeans were heirs of what has been called 'Aramaic common law'. Here in Mahoza, representatives of both communities now found themselves sharing the same geographical space, after several centuries of largely separate existence, and they still understood the provisions of each other's legal documents because they both derived from the same ancient tradition. Even several years after the Roman annexation some documents were written in the Nabataean script, even for agreements between two Jews, despite the fact that Greek documents were already being issued by the Mahoza registry.[5]

If Mahoza had its own registry, we can assume that most villages of comparable size in the Nabataean kingdom also had one – an impressive and wide-ranging administrative network. The basic definition of each property, as set out in a purchase document, was in terms of who (or what) bordered it on every side – east, west, south and north, usually in that order – an ancient practice with origins in Mesopotamia and which lasted at least into the medieval period. In the early documents, the neighbouring landowners were all Nabataeans; later ones show a mixture of Nabataean and Jewish neighbours. All purchase documents also defined irrigation rights in careful detail. In terrain

as arid as this, it was essential that access to water resources should be organized in an orderly manner to avoid disputes. So, water rights for the date orchard that Simon bought from 'Abi'adan are stated as 'including its irrigation ditches and its [assigned] times of irrigation, one half hour every first day of the week, every week, in perpetuity'. In a later document, drawn up after the Roman annexation, the old Nabataean water rights clearly remain in place: 'on the first day of the week, one half hour from the waters of the wadi [undoubtedly today's Wadi Hasa, with its unfailing waters], together with the heirs of [Simon the] Clothier, and on the second day of the week one half hour out of three allotted shares of water'. Perhaps their meticulous allocation of water rights was one of the aspects that Strabo had so admired in the Nabataeans who, he wrote, because they were 'exceedingly well governed,... in every way kept peace with one another'.

Simon was also guaranteed the right 'to buy and to sell and to pledge as security, and to inherit and to grant as a gift, and to do with these purchases whatever he wishes, from the day the deed was written and in perpetuity'. Numerous catch-all phrases were introduced at every point, to ensure that no aspect of the

THE YEAR-ROUND FLOW OF WADI HASA HAS, SINCE ANTIQUITY, PROVIDED IRRIGATION FOR CROPS AND WATER FOR DOMESTIC PURPOSES. IN NABATAEAN TIMES, FARMERS WERE GIVEN A STRICT ALLOCATION OF TIMES WHEN THEY COULD IRRIGATE FROM 'THE WATERS OF THE WADI'.

agreement could be left uncovered. Thus Simon was entitled to 'every thing whatsoever, small or large, which is fitting for him in respect of these purchases, both in sunny areas and where shadow falls'; at the same time he was protected from any kind of appeal or claim on the property 'from every man from far and near'. The terms of these contracts are the obverse of those of the Hegra inscriptions, in that they show the positive side of the law – the rights that were guaranteed – rather than the negative prohibitions which are more in evidence in Hegra. But other clauses are identical – such as, should Simon fail to meet his legal obligations in the purchase, he would be liable to a fine, part to be paid to the vendor and part 'to our lord Rabbel the king as is customary'.

In this well ordered society Simon prospered, acquiring more land as the years went by. In due course he married Miriam, daughter of Joseph son of Menasseh, and a daughter was born to them whom they named Babatha. We do not know in what year she was born, but it was probably very close to the Roman annexation of Nabataea in AD 106. Life must have changed profoundly for Simon and Miriam – not only did they have new responsibilities of parenthood with their first (and, as it turned out, only) child, but at the same time they had suddenly to ride a roller-coaster of political and legal changes. For a start, ownership of the neighbouring date grove 'of our lord Rabbel the king' was now in the name of 'our lord Caesar', the Roman emperor. But more important was the new Roman legal system they had to grapple with, which was now available alongside the existing Nabataean system.

All Simon's intelligence and ingenuity would have been needed to keep pace with the changes in legal practice, and to figure out how they affected his family and his property in the new and uncharted world of the Roman province of Arabia. Some changes were only to be expected – like part of the fine for the breach of a contract, which previously went to the Nabataean king, now going instead 'to our lord the emperor as is customary'. As for the method of dating a document, since the year could no longer be reckoned by how long a king had ruled, it was now dated by who the Roman consuls were at the time – just names to the residents of the province, for these important people mostly stayed in Rome. Sometimes the year was stated by the length of time the emperor had ruled; but it was easier for Simon to understand when the scribes also wrote how many years it was since the establishment of the new province. Then there were the newfangled Roman names for the months, plus their 'kalends' and 'nones' and 'ides', though at least the scribes usually added the Macedonian names as well, and these were familiar as they had been around since the time of Alexander the Great. Only rarely did they write the Semitic months now – the same in both Nabataean and Jewish calendars – as they had in Rabbel's time. It all took a bit of getting used to.

Language was a problem too. Despite some differences between the Nabataean and Jewish forms of Aramaic, they were mutually comprehensible, at least when spoken; but now Greek was the language of government in the new province, and most official documents were written in it. This was not so hard on Simon and other Jews, who were used to it from the Roman province of Judaea; bilingual Jewish scribes – whose Greek, it has to be admitted, like that of Germanos, was adequate rather than educated – could find employment in a local registry. But for the Arabic-speaking, Aramaic-writing Nabataeans, writing Greek was a skill most of them had yet to acquire.

According to a fourth century Syrian historian, Ammianus Marcellinus, the new province of Arabia was 'compelled to obey our laws by the Emperor Trajan'. In fact, the Roman legal system may not have been imposed by force, but simply made available as an alternative to the existing system; and Nabataean laws may only have been deliberately replaced if they ran counter to Roman ones. Roman courts with their Roman laws were now accessible to all who lived there; they may have replaced those of the Nabataeans as quickly as they did, not because they were more generous, but simply because most people saw them as more authoritative. For important cases, contracts drawn up in Greek under Roman law had more chance of being upheld by Roman courts – anyone who wanted to be part of the Roman system had to adopt Roman procedures.

If a document was written in Nabataean or Aramaic the matter would have to be dealt with according to the existing local system. Thus, documents relating to minor deals involving local residents might still be written in Nabataean, even when neither party was Nabataean – and even several years after the Roman annexation, since any problems could be easily dealt with under local law. In one of the Nabataean documents Babatha's second husband, Judah son of Eleazar Khthusion, took a lease on a palm grove from a fellow-Jew, buying futures on its date crop for three consecutive years and agreeing to pay for the crop of the year 120 in 119, and so on up to the crop of 122. What is odd is that Babatha kept this document at all. The deal had been done some years before she and Judah were married, and the lease had expired – perhaps it had been renewed and the renewal document lost.

Despite Babatha's obvious intelligence, it was clearly not deemed necessary for her to be able to read or write. But 'Abi'adan daughter of Aftah, the Nabataean woman from whom Babatha's father had bought a property in AD 99, was at least sufficiently literate to sign her own name in the Nabataean script on the bill of sale. Illiteracy was no impediment to Babatha's being seen as a highly desirable bride, and her father would have looked for a match from the same social and economic stratum of society that he himself occupied. In Jewish and Roman law a girl reached maturity at the age of 12 years and one day, but it was not uncommon for her to be married while still a minor. We do not know Babatha's age on her first marriage, but it is unlikely that she was more than 15. Nor is it clear in which year she married Jesus son of Jesus though, as we shall see, it may have been in AD 120.

husband's brother Joseph, despite the family's wealth. Further-more, the two guardians, 'appointed four months ago and more', had given her only a derisory two *denarii* per month, and for this reason she now petitioned the governor to order them to produce a better return on the capital. Babatha was evidently granted the right to pursue the case, for on 11 October 125 she issued a summons against the Jewish guardian, John son of Eglas, 'to attend at the court of the governor Julius Julianus in Petra, the metropolis of Arabia', to explain why he had not paid his share of the maintenance 'just as 'Abd'obodas son of Illouthas, your [Nabataean] colleague, has given by receipt'.

On the same day Babatha filed a deposition against both guardians – which, we are told, was written for her 'by request, because of her being illiterate'. In it she claimed that the two *denarii* per month that she had received from them – only 0.5 per cent per month of the total inheritance! – was totally inadequate to keep her son in 'a style of life which befits him'. Therefore she proposed that the capital sum should be given to her to manage, with her own more than equal property standing as security. She would then invest it more rewardingly, to provide three times the interest on the capital that the guardians were producing – 1.5 per cent, or six *denarii*, per month – 'wherewith my son may be raised in splendid style, rendering thanks to these most blessed times of the governorship of Julius Julianus... Otherwise this deposition will serve as documentary evidence of your profiteering from the money of the orphan.'

Illiterate Babatha may have been; innumerate she was not, and she could recognize bad management (or a scam) when she saw it. She was clearly aware that Roman law required that maintenance money should be in line with the family's social and economic status, and also that it permitted recourse to as elevated a person as the provincial governor should a guardian default in his payments. And she (or her lawyer) had a nifty way with words, by turn accusatory against the guardians and ingratiating towards the governor. It was a feisty attempt on Babatha's part to take a greater share of the control of her son's life (and his property) into her own hands – but it did not work. The two guardians continued in their role.

THE 600-SEAT THEATRE INSIDE THE GREAT TEMPLE IN PETRA. IF THIS BUILDING WAS NOT A TEMPLE, BUT SECULAR, THIS MAY HAVE BEEN WHERE THE *BOULE* (CITY COUNCIL) OF PETRA MET TO APPOINT GUARDIANS FOR BABATHA'S ORPHAN SON.

It is in these two documents against the guardians, dated 11 October 125, that Babatha's second husband makes his first appearance, acting as her *epitropos*, or legal representative.[9] In the Hegra inscriptions there is no trace of anyone acting on behalf of a woman; all appear to act in their own right. So too, in the Nabataean documents in Babatha's archive, dated AD 94 and 99, the Nabataean women property owners needed no legal representative in making their contracts. And in her father Simon's deed of gift to his wife Miriam – in Aramaic, so coming under local law – there is no sign of an *epitropos*, or equivalent, acting for Miriam. An *epitropos* occurs only in the Greek documents, under Roman law. In the Roman provinces a local woman (unless she was both a Roman citizen and the mother of three or more children) had to have a man acting on her behalf in any business transaction or legal proceeding. This role was usually filled by the woman's husband, if she had one; if not any man would do, but preferably a relative. Judah son of Eleazar Khthusion is not referred to here as her husband, but he may well have been – unfortunately the date on her marriage contract to him fell victim to an ancient and hungry moth, thus depriving us of the means of confirmation.

Babatha's careful filing of the contract, or *ketubba*, of her marriage to Judah was for the simple reason that her bride money had not been paid over to her after his death a few years later. It is written in Aramaic, and is a fairly standard Jewish *ketubba* of the period – 'according to the law of Moses and the Judaeans'. Her bride money is set at the substantial sum of 400 *denarii*, in addition to which Judah would provide her 'food, and … clothes and … bed [conjugal rights?], provision fitting for a free woman'.[10] The 400 *denarii* would have been held by Judah who would have had the full right to use it, but it remained Babatha's property and was repayable whenever she asked for it in return for the contract – in other words, if she wanted a divorce. Should Judah die before her, as he did, the bride money should be given to Babatha out of his estate; and if his heirs delayed giving it to her, she should 'dwell in my house and be provided for from my house and from my estate until the time that my heirs wish to give [it] to you'. Since Judah's heirs clearly did not wish to give Babatha her money, she kept her marriage contract as prime documentary evidence against the defaulters. Interestingly, among the signatures on this vital document appears the form of words, 'Babatha daughter of Simon for herself' – this illiterate woman, presumably with an outline to write over, wished to sign her own name on her marriage contract.

Judah had been born in Ein Gedi, where his family owned property, but had moved to Mahoza where his father had acquired more. What we do not learn immediately, but it becomes apparent later, is that Judah already had a wife who was very much alive and from whom he was not divorced – it was this archive that gave the clue to polygamy being more widespread in Jewish society at this time than was previously supposed. This first wife, Miriam, was also from Ein Gedi, though there is some evidence that she too, and also Judah's daughter Shelamzion, may have moved to Mahoza. Either way, in so small a society, in which everyone knew everyone else and had relatives in Ein Gedi, Babatha must have known of this marriage before she became Judah's second wife. Even with its underlying problems, her second marriage appears to have introduced a brief period of relative calm in her life.

Judah, despite his family's considerable land-holding on both shores of the Dead Sea, appears to have had an occasional cash-flow problem. On 6 May 124, 'in Ein Gedi village of lord Caesar', he borrowed 60 *denarii* from Magonius Valens, a Roman centurion, with a family property in Ein Gedi as security. He may have negotiated this loan when about to marry, or newly married to Babatha – perhaps without her knowledge, for it is hard to imagine her approving its terms. Some Roman soldiers, with regular pay and little to spend it on in the provinces, appear to have moonlighted as moneylenders in order to increase the purse they took home at the end of their service. In the loan document the rate of interest is stated as 1 per cent per month (twice the rate that Babatha had received from her son's guardians), but Magonius Valens may also have built a hidden extortion into the deal which, if Judah needed the money badly, he would have had to accept. The original figure inscribed on the papyrus was 40 *denarii*; this was then erased and 60 written in its place – either Judah asked for a bigger loan after the document had been drawn up, or else Magonius suddenly saw the possibility of making an extra 20 *denarii*, plus interest. And if Judah defaulted in his monthly repayments – to be completed by January 125 – Magonius would have the right to a courtyard in Ein Gedi, which belonged to Judah's father Eleazar. Judah did repay the loan, for the same courtyard appears four years later in a deed of gift from him to his daughter Shelamzion.

In AD 127 the governor of the Roman province of Arabia, Titus Aninius Sextius Florentinus,[11] ordered a census to be taken of all residents of the province, who had to give a detailed declaration of the property they owned there for tax purposes. This was not new; the Nabataeans had also collected taxes, but the system may have been different. On 2 December Babatha, again with Judah son of Eleazar Khthusion acting as her *epitropos*, went north-east into the hills, to Rabbath Moab where Priscus the Roman cavalry prefect, or district commander, had his office. There she declared four properties, all date groves, that she owned in Mahoza, for each one giving details of its name, its area (calculated by the amount of barley that could be sown in it – a very ancient practice dating back to Sumerian times), and the quantity of dates (or cash equivalent) that were due as ordinary tax, and also as 'crown tax' (cash only). After Babatha had waited two days at Rabbath Moab – which, being in the highlands and in winter, must have seemed cold to her – Priscus added a note, which was translated from Latin into Greek, saying that he had received her declaration. Five witnesses, all Nabataeans, signed beside the knots on the back of the document. Babatha was then free to go home, down the hill to the pleasant winter warmth of the Dead Sea, taking her precious new document with her. Despite the fact that the inner text clearly stated that the original was displayed in the basilica at Rabbath Moab, she preferred to have a copy in her own hands.

In February 128 Judah had another cash-flow problem. This time, instead of taking a usurious loan from a Roman centurion, he took a 'deposit' of 300 *denarii* from Babatha – here for the first time named as 'his own wife'. Since this legal transaction was with her husband, Babatha had to have someone else acting as her *epitropos*, preferably a family member; so the otherwise unknown Jacob son of Jesus (possibly a brother of Babatha's first husband) was drafted in for the purpose. If Judah had taken a regular loan, there would have been a fixed schedule of repayments built into the document; but with the more flexible concept of a deposit, repayment was left open, 'until such time as it may please Babatha… to request the aforesaid *denarii* of the deposit from the said Judah'. The penalties for failure to repay his wife promptly on request were swingeing:

> in accordance with the law of deposit he shall be liable to repay the deposit to her twofold in addition to damages, … the said Babatha… having the right of execution upon Judah and all his possessions everywhere – both those which he possesses and those which he may validly acquire in addition – in whatever manner the executor may choose to carry out the execution.

Judah may have needed the money to marry off his daughter for, dated only six weeks later, we have the contract of mar-

riage between Shelamzion and another Judah (surnamed Kimber), son of Ananias. Judah Kimber also owned property both in Ein Gedi, his birthplace, and in Mahoza, his place of residence. The bride money on this occasion was 500 *denarii*, of which 200 (in 'feminine adornment in silver and gold and clothing') came from her father, and 300 from the bridegroom – the total suitably higher (but not much) than Babatha's bride money for her second marriage, and testimony to the wealth of both sides of the match. Since the groom had the use of all the bride money, one does wonder what he would have done with 200 *denarii*-worth of 'feminine adornment… and clothing'!

Unlike Babatha's Aramaic *ketubba* of only a few years before, this contract was in Greek and, instead of being 'according to the law of Moses and the Judaeans', it was 'in accordance with Greek custom'. It was the norm in Graeco-Roman cities of the area for the father to give his daughter in marriage, as Judah son of Eleazar does here; in Jewish custom the groom would have initiated the contract – unless the bride was a minor, and there is no indication that this was the case with Shelamzion. This is a quite different type of document from Babatha's *ketubba* – an indication, perhaps, that even for their marriages Jews (and very likely Nabataeans as well) were increasingly using forms of contract that were acceptable in Roman courts. The bridegroom, Judah Kimber, like many of his Nabataean contemporaries, had even adopted a Roman surname, presumably to keep in good odour with the new rulers.

Eleven days later, Judah son of Eleazar drew up a deed of gift in favour of his daughter. In it Shelamzion was given 'all his possessions in Ein Gedi' – the same courtyard that had stood as security for his loan from the Roman centurion four years before. His own father, Eleazar, who owned it in 124, must have died by now and Judah was the rightful owner. But he did not give Shelamzion the property outright – she could have 'half of the courtyard… including half the rooms and the upper storey rooms' immediately, and the other half after his death, from which moment she could hold it 'validly and securely for all time, to build, raise up, raise higher, excavate, deepen, possess, use, sell and manage in whatever manner she may choose, all valid and secure'. He also promised that 'whenever Shelamzion summons the said Judah [her father] he will register it with the public authorities'.

Shelamzion's deed of gift – perhaps kept at the urging of her stepmother, Babatha – was filed carefully with Babatha's own documents. Two years later, after the death of both Judah and his

NINE

AFTERGLOW OF EMPIRE

The Nabataeans and Christianity
in the Byzantine Era

AN IMAGINATIVELY CRESTED STORK FROM THE SIXTH CENTURY MOSAIC IN THE NORTH AISLE OF THE PETRA CHURCH.

C USTOMS DUES, BATHS, THEATRES and taxes' – so the first century AD rabbi Gamaliel II, spiritual leader of the Jews, had summed up the draining effect of Roman rule in the provinces. His aphorism may epitomize the Roman policy of both giving to and taking from their new subjects, but it ignores the army, whose pay and upkeep were the main reason for the taxes. Claudius Severus, first governor of the province of Arabia (107–c.115), oversaw the building of forts at strategic points to house the Roman legionaries who came to maintain law and order. In addition, auxiliary units raised in other parts of the empire were brought in; and there were at least six cohorts of Nabataean soldiers – the *Cohortes Ulpiae Petraeorum* (named after the emperor, Marcus Ulpius Traianus) – among which the old royal army was probably included. On their discharge, these Nabataeans would have been rewarded with the honour of Roman citizenship. Once the Via Nova Traiana was completed in AD 114 – from Bostra in the north, via Petra, to the Red Sea port of Aela in the south – the Romans had little difficulty in moving men and arms quickly to wherever they were needed.

In the south, the shape of the new province was broadly the same as that of the old kingdom, stretching from the eastern desert, across Wadi Araba and into the Negev; it included part of the Hejaz, outposts in Wadi Sirhan, and probably the Sinai. The main change was in the north where, with the addition to the province of Arabia of parts of what had once been the Decapolis, the border with Syria now ran from just north of Bostra to an uncertain point east of Lake Tiberias, where the province of Judaea began.

Towns throughout the province flourished, growing larger and grander as centres of Roman administration, trade and wor-ship. Not only were baths and theatres built in them, but temples, basilicas, agoras and colon-naded streets – basic attributes of any self-respecting Graeco-Roman town. Many were given the new classification of *polis*, city, and had a city council, or *boule*, to go with their new sta-tus. Rabbath Moab, where Babatha filed her land declaration, was one of several so hon-oured; later it was given the Greek name Areopolis.

Petra and Bostra were in a separate category. For long they had been the two major centres in the Nabataean kingdom and, in the reign of the last two kings, perhaps shared the role of cap-ital, depending on where the king was. Petra's designation as *metropolis*, 'mother city', soon after the annexation of the king-dom, was commemorated in an inscription of AD 114 found in the colonnaded street. Bostra was honoured by the emperor in another way, receiving his own name, Nea Traiane Bostra – Trajan's new Bostra – which reflected his active involvement in initiating the recreation of the city. Bostra had obvious advan-tages – the rich agricultural lands that surrounded it, which had been greatly developed during the reigns of Malichus II and Rabbel II, and the network of new imperial trade routes of which it was the focal point. But it clearly needed to be brought up to a standard that matched the imperial name. In 130 Trajan's successor, Hadrian, named Petra after himself – Hadriane Petra – and under Severus Alexander (222–235) both cities were ele-vated to the status of colony.

THE BLACK BASALT THEATRE AT BOSTRA, PROBABLY DATING TO THE LATE SECOND CENTURY AD, WAS BUILT DURING THE ROMAN RECONSTRUCTION OF THE CITY AFTER THE ANNEXATION OF THE NABATAEAN KINGDOM.

Whatever there had been of Nabataean Bostra was used to build the new and glorious Roman city that grew in its place. Baths, colonnaded streets, arches, a hippodrome, agora and basilica, and the vast black basalt theatre, were built at various times in the second to third centuries. In this new and imposing city, in 247, the Emperor Philip the Arab held the Actia Dusaria (see page 126), magnificent Greek-style games for athletes, musicians, jugglers and the like, to celebrate Rome's millennium. The name of the celebrations linked Greek culture with Roman imperial glory, embodied by Augustus' victory at the battle of Actium, and with the still active Nabataean religion, represented by Dushara. For three sleepless days and nights the Bostrans revelled amid the clamour and rich pageantry of the games. In recognition of Bostra's elevated role, Philip also gave the city the coveted status of *metropolis*.

Petra was already magnificent. Apart from some repair work that was necessitated by the earthquake of 113/114 —

such as reconstructing part of the theatre, and doubtless some other buildings as well — its glories needed little embellishment. Its continuing prosperity ensured that it stayed that way. A Roman touch was added by building a Trajanic arch, complete with inscription, and perhaps by repaving the street to connect with the Via Nova; but there were no major structural changes in the city after the end of the Nabataean kingdom. The main changes were administrative and, as Babatha's archive shows, Petra quickly developed all the institutions of a Graeco-Roman city, with its city council and governor's court, and its public archives in the temple of Aphrodite.

In the Negev the Romans at first maintained the ancient trade route, reconstructing sections of it in stone, putting up milestones, rebuilding most of the forts that protected it, and restoring the caravanserais. The Nabataean sites in the Negev had so far remained non-residential. Not even Oboda was a place of settled residence, though its large army camp and its temples made it both an important military base for the protection of caravans and a centre of worship for the surrounding tribes. Only Elusa had a theatre dating from the late Nabataean period, which may indicate a settled population. It was probably not until the reign of Diocletian (284–305) that people started to settle at other places in the Negev, residential quarters began to be built, and these sites became urban centres.

Also under Diocletian a new and easier road was built in the northern Negev. With no serious enemy against whom to defend the trade route, the Romans did not need the natural protection of difficult terrain that the Nabataeans had adopted.

Their new road climbed from Wadi Araba to the western highlands by what is today called the Scorpions' Pass, then ran past a minor Nabataean base called Kurnub (known as Mampsis in the Byzantine period, today's Mamshit), and from there passed through easy, open territory via Beersheba to the coast. Kurnub was now transformed into a major town – the only one in the Negev to be enclosed by a wall – and, as the new road drew traffic from the old southern route, so Oboda declined and Kurnub became the new centre of the Negev. It was not in the most promising agricultural terrain and the local Nabataeans, with their knowledge of the land and expertise in water control, must have laughed silently as they watched the Romans building a series of three great dams in the wadi beside the new town. Perhaps they were hired as local labour, taking their Roman pay and sharing the joke at home. Maybe the dams produced a short-lived agricultural revolution; but they soon silted up and all that labour was lost.

ONE OF A SERIES OF THREE DAMS BUILT NEAR KURNUB BY THE ROMANS (A SECOND ONE CAN BE SEEN HIGHER UP THE WADI). IF THEY HAD ASKED ADVICE OF THE NABATAEANS, WHO WERE BRILLIANT HYDRAULIC ENGINEERS, THE ROMANS WOULD DOUBTLESS NOT HAVE BUILT ANYTHING SO GRANDIOSE AND USELESS – THE DAMS SOON SILTED UP.

THE SCANTY REMAINS OF A TEMPLE AT OBODA, PERHAPS THAT DEDICATED TO 'OBODAS THE GOD', IN MEMORY OF THE GREAT NABATAEAN KING OF THE EARLY FIRST CENTURY BC, OBODAS I.

STAIRS INSIDE THE ROMAN MILITARY TOWER, BUILT AT OBODA IN AD 293. AN INSCRIPTION ON THE LINTEL OVER THE ENTRANCE TO THE TOWER INVOKED THE HELP OF ZEUS-OBODAS, A REFERENCE TO THE STILL POPULAR NABATAEAN GOD-KING, OBODAS I.

At Oboda a temple, probably built in the reign of Rabbel II, was rededicated in 268 to Zeus-Obodas. Other dedications to Aphrodite and Apis indicate that there was more than one temple on the acropolis of this ancient site, but the deified King Obodas clearly remained a focal point in the worship of the place that had taken his name. Apart from the temple dedication, several other inscriptions invoking 'Zeus-Obodas' or 'Obodas the god' have been found, including one in Greek from the time of Diocletian on the lintel of a Roman military tower: 'To Good Fortune. O Zeus-Obodas, help Eirenaios, building the tower with good omens in the year 188 [AD 293/4], with Ouaelos the builder, a Petraean.'

Ouaelos the builder, with his Nabataean name and specified place of origin, demonstrates the survival of the old ways and the old names; we can only guess at the Greek-named Eirenaios' ethnic origin. It had for a long time been fashionable for Nabataeans and other residents of the area to adopt a name that identified with the prevalent Hellenistic culture. In the reign of the emperor Gallienus (259–268) two sophists from Petra called Callinicus and Genethlius were probably also Nabataeans, but their origins have been hidden behind the same Hellenizing screen. They were distinguished enough to practise rhetoric in the very heart of the Greek cultural world, Athens. They were not the only men from the old Nabataean kingdom who were outstanding in the field of Greek culture and learning – the Negev town of Elusa was the birthplace of the great rhetorician Zenobius, who went on to become the sophist of Antioch in Syria in the early fourth century. As professor of rhetoric there, he taught the philosopher and writer Libanius, the most renowned man of letters of his age.

These sophists were denizens of the Roman world, free to travel wherever their talents and their imagination would take them, for after the collapse in 135 of Bar Kokhba's revolt, the whole Roman Empire enjoyed an extended period of peace and reliable law and order. According to the orator Aelius Aristides, a resident of Smyrna in the Roman province of Asia:

> Wars have so far vanished as to be legendary affairs of the
> past…A man simply travels from one country to another
> as though it were his native land. We are no longer fright-
> ened by… the narrow sandy tracks that lead from Arabia
> into Egypt. We are not dismayed by the height of moun-
> tains… or by inhospitable tribes of barbarians. To be a
> Roman citizen, nay even one of your subjects, is a suffi-
> cient guarantee of personal safety.[1]

For Christian subjects, however, personal safety was considerably less guaranteed. Since the time of Jesus of Nazareth his followers had evolved a distinctive way of life and thought, underlined by their New Testament, their rule of faith and their liturgy. Although originally seen by the pagan majority as a deviant Jewish sect, the only thing Christians shared with the Jews was their monotheism and its concomitant abhorrence of idolatry. Gradually they were seen as a disturbing category all their own, with an efficient organization behind them, a hierarchy of bishops, presbyters and deacons, an impressive mutual support system among the laity, and a reputation for helping others in times of plague or barbarian raids. Their numbers continued to grow.

All this was viewed with deep suspicion not only by officials who were committed to maintaining the sanctity of the Roman gods and of the emperor, but also by increasing sections of non-official society. Christians were regarded as irreligious, bent on undermining the ancient polytheistic traditions and attacking the accepted divine status of the emperor, from whom all blessings of peace and prosperity flowed. The extreme threat that they were deemed to pose to civilized society resulted in accusations against them of depraved morals of the most lurid kind, incest, cannibalism, 'atheism', and lack of patriotism; and the blame for any misfortune that occurred – drought, famine, plague, floods – was laid at their door.

Trajan, and even Hadrian, had tried to keep the worst anti-Christian excesses in check by insisting that no punishment might be inflicted without the accused person being properly charged and the case heard in an accredited court. To do otherwise, Trajan said, would be 'not in keeping with the spirit of the age'. But the tide of anti-Christian feeling gathered strength, and succeeding emperors – even the virtuous and high-minded Marcus Aurelius – were swept along with it. Edicts were issued disbanding Christian groups, confiscating property, dismissing Christians from official positions, or forcing everyone to get a certificate from the magistrate testifying that they had sacrificed to the gods. Although implementation of these edicts was patchy, and there were periods of respite and reasonable coexistence, there were also times of brutal persecution. Then provincial governors would be hold trials of Christians who had been hunted down by city officials and soldiers with the help of census lists – all levels of society were involved in rooting them out. Anyone who refused to recant and sacrifice to the Roman gods was condemned to torture or death, and often both.

But if some emperors, or enraged mobs, thought they could wipe out the Christian disease with executions and torture they were mistaken. Although many Christians rushed to sacrifice to the Roman gods to save their lives, many others chose the most terrible forms of death rather than deny their faith. The waves of persecutions – at their worst in the reigns of Septimius Severus (193–211), Decius (249–251), Diocletian (284–305) and Galerius (305–311) – did not achieve the desired elimination of Christian belief. On the contrary, the numbers of believers kept multiplying.

All this bigotry must have seemed deeply regrettable to those tolerant Nabataeans for whom religious syncretism was a way of life. For a long time their gods had been assimilated with those of Greece and Egypt, and identifications with Roman counterparts were already in place well before the Roman takeover. Most Nabataeans needed no imperial orders to sacrifice to Dushara in the guise of Jupiter, or to al-'Uzza under the name of either Aphrodite or Venus. For these, martyrdom did not enter their lives. Yet Petra also had its Christians who refused to submit to Diocletian's decrees. They were persecuted by the authorities, in particular by the prefect Maximus whose enthusiasm for the job was so outstanding that he was sent to go and do likewise in Philadelphia (Amman), and promoted to the governorship of the province.[2] Also within Nabataean territory, Christians were condemned to work in the copper mines of Phaeno (present-day Feinan), where they were shackled, mutilated and held under ruthless military supervision. Many died. While most of those condemned to the mines came from Egypt or Palestine, some were doubtless Nabataeans.

PART OF THE ROMAN/BYZANTINE REMAINS OF FEINAN, WHERE CHRISTIANS WERE SENT TO WORK THE COPPER MINES IN THE SURROUNDING HILLS.

On the official level, it was not in the Nabataeans' interests to have any argument with Diocletian – indeed, they put up dedications and monuments in his honour in Petra and elsewhere. And Diocletian did some good things. His orderly mind wanted to see everything working in harmony, though naturally under his own control. He reorganized the taxation system of the entire empire, which may not have been as popular as his officials tried to make it sound; and he issued an edict regulating market prices for goods and services, which may have pleased householders rather more than traders. Most wide-ranging of all was his reorganization in the 290s of the whole Roman Empire, with the ultimate purpose of reducing the power of the provincial governors. He divided supreme rule between four tetrarchs: two senior emperors – himself in the fast-developing east, the other in the west – and two subordinate Caesars. In the east he transferred the southern part of the province of Arabia to the province of Syria Palaestina which, around the end of the fourth century, became a separate province, Palaestina Tertia, with Petra as its capital. By this time Petra was at least partially Christian, and the seat of a metropolitan bishop.

In 313 the co-emperors of west and east, Constantine and Licinius, had issued a joint edict enjoining religious tolerance and giving official recognition and security to Christians. It was probably a shrewd rather than a committed move – despite persecution, Christians were now the strongest and best-organized group in the empire; if they were brought onto the imperial side, what might not be achieved? But in little over a decade the two emperors had fallen out; in 324 Constantine defeated Licinius and reigned alone over the reunited empire. Soon afterwards he decided to transfer his capital from Rome to Byzantium, which was given his own name: Constantinople, the city of Constantine. As Diocletian had already recognized, the emphasis of the empire had shifted eastwards – the newest provinces, with the wealth they brought to the imperial coffers, lay east of the Mediterranean, and many old ones in the west had been lost to the Goths. Under Constantine's rule Christianity became the most favoured religion, with the emperor as God's vicegerent on earth, the thirteenth apostle. By the end of the fourth century it had become the state religion throughout the Roman empire.

The Christian Church had from its inception been a proselytizing community, urging on non-believers the need for conversion. Now at last they were free to preach their good news of salvation through Christ without fear of persecution. The late-fourth-century scholar Jerome, in his hagiography of St

Hilarion,[3] tells of the extraordinary success of this saint in winning souls. Around 350 St Hilarion went with a band of fellow-monks to visit one of his disciples in Elusa,[4] a town dedicated to the cult of the goddess Venus, in the form of the morning star. By chance he arrived on the very day of a great festival in honour of the goddess, when all her devotees in the region were gathered at her temple. Hilarion had already acquired an enviable reputation for miraculous cures and casting out demons, and the assembled crowd of men, women and children, not wishing to let slip the opportunity of his presence among them, swarmed out to meet him and begged him for a blessing. By this they probably did not mean that he should make them Christians – but this was what happened, and with such spectacular success that the people would not let him leave the city until he had drawn in the earth the plan of their new church and marked the priest of Venus with the sign of the cross. Thus, according to the eulogizing Jerome, did Christianity come to Elusa.

Although Christianity did indeed take root in Elusa, and its own bishop was appointed, pagan worship was not eliminated. Nor did the new religion have any noticeable effect on the buying and selling of slaves there. Near the end of the fourth century Nilus, a rich and well-born Constantinopolitan, who had become a hermit at Mount Sinai, wrote of a raid by some Venus-worshipping 'Saracens' in which several Sinai monks were killed. Nilus' son, Theodoulos, was captured by the raiders, who planned to sacrifice him to their goddess at that moment before dawn when Venus appeared on the horizon. Luckily for Theodoulos, his captors drank so much wine the night before that they failed to rise until the sun had risen, thus missing the propitious moment for his sacrifice. Instead, they sold him as a slave to a man from Elusa. Nilus appealed to the bishop of Elusa, who redeemed Theodoulos and ordained both father and son as priests, after which the two saints heroically returned to the Sinai to carry on their interrupted missionary work.

From this time on, increasing numbers of churches were built in all the major centres of the erstwhile Nabataean kingdom, and throughout the empire. With succeeding emperors assuming the role of God's representative on earth and combining both temporal and spiritual powers, so the Church represented the empire in the provinces, with the clergy in the role of imperial clerks. Contributions from Constantinople towards building magnificent churches in outlying regions – far bigger and more numerous than the local populations required – were regarded as investments for maintaining the emperor's power.

A RECONSTRUCTED NABATAEAN FARM AT SOBATA (TODAY'S SHIVTA) IN THE NEGEV. BOTH HERE AND AT OBODA (AVDAT) THE OLD TERRACES AND WATER CHANNELS WERE RESTORED AS PART OF EXPERIMENTAL WORK IN THE 1960S BY PROFESSOR MICHAEL EVEN-ARI OF THE HEBREW UNIVERSITY IN JERUSALEM AND A TEAM OF BOTANISTS AND AGRARIANS. IT WAS DISCOVERED THAT EACH PLOT OF LAND NEEDED ON AVERAGE 20 TIMES ITS SIZE AS A WATER CATCHMENT AREA FOR IRRIGATION.

The population of the empire grew so rapidly that people increasingly moved into semi-desert areas – places that even the Nabataeans had considered unrewarding for human habitation when gentler alternatives were available. Thus the Negev, peripheral until now apart from the trade route, became a major growth area. Nabataeans as well as other Arabs from the region settled, built houses, terraced the wadi beds, and developed elaborate systems of channels on the hillsides to bring water to the terraces. It was a huge labour – each plot of cultivated land required about 20 times its size as a catchment area for irrigation. Since such agriculture could not possibly sustain a large population, subsidies and imported food supplies were provided by the Church on behalf of the empire. The churches were not only major landowners, they also provided an effective administrative and legal network that operated at every level of society, and reached even the remotest of the newly populated areas.

The veneration of sites connected with Jesus, the apostles and Old Testament patriarchs and prophets had begun almost as soon as the persecutions were over. So too had the cult of martyrs killed in the persecutions. As pilgrims could now travel safely in most parts of the empire, churches throughout the Nabataean lands, as elsewhere, scrambled to acquire relics of well known martyrs in order to become centres of pilgrimage (and so increase their income). The Negev was particularly successful as the main routes from Jerusalem to Mount Sinai passed through it. Splendid churches were built in the second half of the fourth century at Oboda, Sobata and Kurnub/Mampsis – and probably also at Elusa, but the extent of the destruction, and

ONE OF THE MANGERS IN A LARGE STABLE AT KURNUB/MAMPSIS. THE NEGEV MAY HAVE BECOME AN AREA OF HORSE-BREEDING DURING THE BYZANTINE PERIOD. STABLES WERE ALSO FOUND AT SOBATA.

THE NEGEV BECAME A WINE-PRODUCING AREA IN THE BYZANTINE PERIOD. INSTEAD OF EACH PRODUCER HAVING HIS OWN SMALL WINEPRESS, LARGE COMMUNAL ONES WERE MADE, LIKE THIS ONE AT OBODA, WITH SEPARATE SECTIONS AROUND THE TREADING AREA SO THAT EACH FARMER COULD UNLOAD HIS GRAPES INTO HIS OWN SECTION AND WAIT HIS TURN FOR TREADING.

the lack of full excavation, make it impossible to know as yet. The one church so far excavated there appears to date to the mid-fifth century, as do the churches built in Nessana in the far south of the Negev. Petra, too, became an early place of pilgrimage thanks to its association with the death and burial of Aaron, brother of Moses; it also boasted a cluster of local martyrs to whom churches, chapels and hospitals were dedicated, both in the capital itself and in outlying towns and villages.

During the periods of persecution, Christians had had no time to discuss nuances of doctrine; in any case their survival had depended on unity. Once freed from these constraints, dormant theological problems quickly surfaced and doctrinal dif-

ferences began to emerge. Disputes, originally local, spread widely and protagonists of both sides became locked in bitter controversy. In 325 the Emperor Constantine, assuming the mantle of patron of the Christian church, summoned his bishops to the First Ecumenical Council at Nicaea (now Iznik). The main item on the agenda was a dispute between Bishop Alexander of Alexandria, supported by his controversial young deacon Athanasius, and Arius, a learned presbyter in the diocese, over whether Jesus was 'of one substance with the Father', and therefore equal; Arius had claimed that because Jesus was 'begotten of the Father' he must be subordinate. The Council's condemnation of Arius' view led to a polarization between the orthodox camp and those who disagreed – however saintly and sincere the dissenters might be, they were dubbed heretics. The Christian church was supposed to speak with one voice only.

The bishop of Petra was not listed as a participant in the Council of Nicaea, but Bishop Asterius of 'Petra in Arabia' was at the Synod of Sardica (Sofia) in 343 to discuss once again the Arian heresy which had refused to go away. While most of the

THE NORTH CHURCH AT
SOBATA, BUILT IN THE LATE
FOURTH CENTURY. THE THICK
DEFENSIVE WALLS WERE BUILT
SOME TIME LATER TO
WITHSTAND POSSIBLE ATTACKS BY
SARACENS.

THE HANDSOME CRUCIFORM BAPTISMAL FONT OF THE LATE-FOURTH-CENTURY
SOUTH CHURCH AT SOBATA WOULD HAVE BEEN IN A MORE OPEN AREA IN THE
PERIOD OF ITS USE. INITIATES WOULD DESCEND INTO THE WATER ON ONE SIDE,
HAVE WATER POURED OVER THEIR HEADS BY THE PRIEST FROM THE SMALL BASIN
AT THE SIDE, AND EMERGE ON THE OTHER SIDE AS NEW MEMBERS OF THE
CHRISTIAN CHURCH.

Nabataean Christian inhabitants of the diocese of Petra may
well have been bemused at such religious wrangling, their bishop
actively took up the cudgels on their behalf. Asterius was originally pro-Arian, but then defected to the orthodox side, led by
Athanasius, now bishop of Alexandria. The new emperor,
Constantine's son Constantius II, was sympathetic to the Arians
who persuaded him to exile Asterius to Libya where he was
'treated with insult', and to replace him with the pro-Arian
Germanus. In 361 everything changed again when Julian, who
had converted back to paganism, became emperor for two years.
In an act of apparent toleration he recalled all exiled bishops,
including Asterius who took part in the unifying Synod of
Alexandria in 362 under the leadership of Athanasius, who had

also been recalled from exile. Whether good relations would have
lasted between the Christians and their pagan emperor may be
doubted – Christianity was firmly entrenched throughout the
empire, while the last bastions of paganism struggled for survival. Tension was inevitable. In the end the question never arose
– in 363 the rebuilding, authorized by Julian, of the Jewish temple in Jerusalem was brought to a catastrophic end by explosions
and fire, probably related to the devastating earthquake of 19
May; and five weeks later the emperor was killed in battle against
the Persians. It must have struck many Christians as a double,
and on balance felicitous, act of God.

Although Eusebius, the ecclesiastical historian, reported
that in Constantine's reign churches were being built in Petra
(presumably by converted Nabataeans), the old religion still kept
many devotees. It was doubtless these to whom Eusebius referred
when he wrote that Petra was 'filled with superstitious men, who
have sunk in diabolical error'. So life in Petra continued, with
Christians and pagans worshipping side by side in the heart of
their city.

A strange tale is told by St Epiphanios, bishop of Salamis
in Cyprus in the late fourth century, of a ritual of rebirth, apparently connected with a sun goddess, that occurred in Petra every
year on the night of 5-6 January – coincidentally his own name-
day feast of Epiphany. After an all-night vigil filled with hymns
and flute music, at cock-crow the celebrants entered a shrine by
torchlight and brought up the statue of a goddess. This they
processed around the heart of the temple just before sunrise, to
the accompaniment of flutes, kettle-drums and hymns, 'calling
her in Arabic "Chaamu", which means... "virgin"; and the one
born from her they call "Dusares", which means "only begotten
of the Lord"'. Epiphanios adds that the same ritual took place
in Elusa; and both the Petra and Elusa manifestations were based
on the festival held in Alexandria on the same night.[5] While this
might appear as a blatant case of Nabataean syncretism, trying
to keep everyone happy with Nabataean gods being assimilated
with the story of the birth of Jesus, it is more likely that
Epiphanios was allowing his zeal for finding pagan parallels of
Jesus' virgin birth to colour his imagination. In any case, it shows
pagan worship alive and well in Petra in the late fourth century.

Freedom from persecution had not only opened the way
for doctrinal disputes among Christians, it also gave some
unsavoury characters a licence to persecute pagans in their turn.
Among them was Barsauma, a Syrian monk whose extreme
asceticism led him to eat nothing but fruits and roots (in sum-

mer, only on alternate days), and to wear an iron tunic so that he froze in winter and roasted in summer. His already bizarre appearance was reinforced by hair that reached his feet, and he was reputed never to sit or lie down, day or night. Combining these uncomfortable forms of Christian zeal with the talents of a gang-leader, he and a mob of 40 like-minded companions travelled around the empire destroying pagan temples and Jewish synagogues. Around 423 they reached Petra, but the inhabitants had had prior warning of their arrival and shut the gates against them. Barsauma's demands that he and his gang be let in, accompanied by threats of attack and conflagration if they were not, forced the Petraeans to reconsider their position. They let them in. There had been an unbroken drought in the region for four years, and we can imagine the total disbelief that must have met Barsauma's next move — an announcement that it was going to rain. At this point there was so intense a deluge that parts of the city walls were broken down — an occurrence of such truly miraculous significance that the priests of al-'Uzza and Dushara were prompted to convert at once to Barsauma's obviously more efficacious religion.[6]

Whether or not 'Saint' Barsauma and his band of thugs were quite as successful as they advertised themselves to be, there is no doubt that Christianity became the predominant religion of the Nabataean population of Petra during the fifth century.

AERIAL VIEW OF JABAL HAROUN; ON THE SADDLE BELOW ARE THE REMAINS OF A MONASTIC CHURCH DEDICATED TO 'ST AARON', IN THE PROCESS OF EXCAVATION.

By now churches were popping up all over the city. Either in the late fourth century or the early fifth, a small church was built on the ridge overlooking the northern approach to the city, and a large monastic complex, dedicated to 'St Aaron', was built just below the summit of Jabal Haroun (Mount Aaron). In July 446 the cavernous interior of the Urn Tomb was consecrated for Christian worship, the recesses at the eastern end having been carved into the form of a main apse and two side apses, and a roughly square chancel area marked out with low marble screens. In one corner an inscription was painted directly onto the sandstone wall: 'In the time of the most holy bishop Jason this place was dedicated… to Christ the Saviour.'

THE RIDGE CHURCH, BUILT IN THE LATE FOURTH OR EARLY FIFTH CENTURY AD ON A HILL OVERLOOKING THE CENTRE OF PETRA; UMM AL-BIYARA IS IN THE BACKGROUND.

Sometime before the end of the fifth century, a large triple-aisled church was built on the hillside immediately north of the colonnaded street, with a single central apse at the east end and an atrium on the west. Little of the original interior remains, except the handsome mosaic floor in most of the south aisle, depicting human and allegorical figures, animals and birds in a geometric frame. The complex also included a baptistery just west of the atrium. The large cruciform baptismal font, sunk into a raised platform with a column at each corner, has steps in all four arms of the cross for initiates to descend into the water on one side, each in turn, have water poured over their heads by the officiating priest from the small basin set into the platform, and emerge on the other side as new members of Christ's Church. The narrowness of the steps would have precluded all but skinny initiates. In the early days of Christian liberation baptism had been primarily for adults who had converted from their earlier pagan beliefs; in time these converts brought their children to be baptized, or even infants, for whom the small basin alone would have been used.

The scale and elaboration of this church complex indicates that Petra had continued to flourish, even after the earthquake of 363. Most structures that were damaged then had probably been restored; those which had remained in their tumbled state now provided convenient building material for new churches. More evidence of prosperity appears a few decades after the original building – a pavement of *opus sectile* work was laid in the central nave, made of costly imported marble (most of which disappeared in antiquity), enlivened with local dark-red sandstone; and yet more marble was used for the finely carved chancel screen, the miniature columns that supported it and altars. The two side aisles had apses made in their east ends, and the whole of the north aisle and the eastern part of the south aisle had mosaic floors laid in them, with birds, animals and human figures in roundels bordered with vines. All the floor mosaics remain; but of those that once adorned the walls and ceilings, executed in tiny glass tesserae, only a few fragments survive. The strict conventions of early Byzantine ecclesiastical art make possible their schematic reconstruction in the mind's eye. The whole purpose was to transform the interior of the church into an image of the cosmos – the floor presented the natural world of God's creation; the lower walls, the world of Christian saints and martyrs; the upper walls, the Holy Land with scenes from Jesus' life; and in the ceiling reigned Christ Pantocrator, the Omnipotent, the image of God Himself.

THE URN TOMB, CARVED FOR
THE BURIAL OF A NABATAEAN
KING (PERHAPS MALICHUS II) IN
THE FIRST CENTURY AD, WAS
CONVERTED INTO A CHURCH IN
JULY 446.

Petra also became involved in the next heresy. It was caused by Archbishop Nestorius of Constantinople who had started his reign in the capital by setting fire to the church of some respected Arians. Then, despite a marked lack of scholarly gifts, Nestorius recklessly took on the theologians. In distinguishing between Jesus' humanity and his divinity, and stressing his human birth, he stripped the Virgin Mary of her title *Theotokos* (God-bearing). Nothing could have been more designed to cause outrage than this demotion of the Virgin. Nestorius and his teachings were condemned by the Third Ecumenical Council at Ephesus in 431, and he was dubbed 'the new Judas', deposed and unfrocked. That night Ephesus resounded with torchlight celebrations and dancing in the streets. Although the bishop of Petra did not sign the condemnation, it was to Petra that Nestorius and some of his fellow-heretics were banished in the autumn of 435; but soon afterwards he was sent into permanent exile to an oasis in the Egyptian desert, where he ended his days.

The swing of the pendulum produced the next heresy, Monophysitism, which maintained that Jesus had a single, wholly divine, nature. The orthodox position, pronounced at the Fourth Ecumenical Council at Chalcedon in 451, was that Jesus was 'truly God and truly man... to be acknowledged in two

THIS VIEW OF THE WHOLE FLOOR AREA OF THE PETRA CHURCH WAS TAKEN
FROM A HOT-AIR BALLOON SOON AFTER COMPLETION OF THE EXCAVATIONS. THE
EARLIER MOSAICS ARE IN THE WESTERN END OF THE SOUTH (RIGHT-HAND)
AISLE. PHOTO BY W. & E. MYERS; REPRODUCED BY COURTESY OF THE
AMERICAN CENTER OF ORIENTAL RESEARCH, AMMAN.

AN AFRICAN CARRYING A VASE, FROM THE SIXTH CENTURY MOSAIC IN THE
NORTH AISLE OF THE PETRA CHURCH.

A MARBLE VASE WITH
HANDLES IN THE SHAPE
OF LIONS, FOUND
DURING EXCAVATIONS
IN THE PETRA CHURCH.
(PETRA MUSEUM)

natures without confusion, without change, without division,
without separation'. For the first time a ruling of an Ecumenical
Council was rejected by large sections of the Christian Church,
and the divisions thus created were never healed. As with
Arianism, succeeding emperors took different positions in the
dispute. Meanwhile, Petra seems to have acquired a bizarre kind
of popularity as a place of exile – for heretics when orthodoxy
or another form of heresy ruled, or for charlatans.

In 512 the Monophysite Emperor Anastasius sent the
Nestorian Patriarch Flavian of Antioch into exile in Petra, and
also another Antiochene called John Isthmeos, an alchemist who,
according to the chronicler John Malalas, was 'a tremendous
impostor'. A few years later Anastasius' heir, the illiterate (but

orthodox) Justin I, sent Mare, the Monophysite bishop of Amida (present-day Diyarbakır in Turkey), 'to a hard and distant place of exile at Petra'.[7] So testing was it that Mare and the deacons and notaries who accompanied him, together with another exiled bishop, were 'in great distress exceeding their power of endurance, until their lives were near disappearing'. Mare therefore sent his deacon, 'the virtuous zealous Stephen', to Constantinople to intercede with 'anyone whom God might put in his way to be able to have that place altered for them'. By chance (or God's design), he gained the ear of the redoubtable

THE DISCOVERY IN DECEMBER 1993 OF A CACHE OF CARBONIZED PAPYRUS SCROLLS IN A ROOM BESIDE THE PETRA CHURCH. EACH SCROLL, OR GROUP OF SCROLLS THAT COULD NOT BE DISENTANGLED, WAS WRAPPED IN FOIL TO PREVENT FURTHER DISINTEGRATION.

Theodora, wife of Justin's nephew and heir apparent, Justinian. Theodora was a powerful influence on her husband, who was already assuming near-imperial status. She was also a Monophysite. Thanks to these connections an order was issued in 523 transferring the place of exile of the two bishops, the deacons and notaries, from Petra to the greater ease of Alexandria, 'and accordingly a great relief and deliverance was effected for these blessed men'.

It is curious that Mare found Petra so hard a place of exile for it was hardly less civilized than Amida; Alexandria, however, still one of the great centres of culture of the Mediterranean, was clearly a more delightful option than either. In Petra, the lavish building and decoration of the great church at just about this time indicate a life that was far from rigorous; and the recently discovered sixth-century papyrus scrolls speak of a city, the capital of the province of Palaestina Tertia, that had a rich economic and social life with flourishing agriculture and active institutions. That trade is not mentioned in the papyri comes as no surprise, since the southern routes had some time earlier dwindled to insignificance. The cast of this archive were clergy and landowners, and productive farmers, growing fruits and grains and making wine. The benefits enjoyed by these fortunate people evidently did not filter down to heretics banished to Petra by the hierarchy of the Church and empire.

The cache of about 140 papyri, found in a storeroom beside the great church in Petra in 1993, were carbonized in a fire that ravaged the church and some adjacent buildings, at the earliest in the late seventh century. While it was their carbonization that preserved them, it has also made the work of conservation and decipherment[8] extraordinarily difficult – it is like working with highly complex jigsaw puzzles, so fragile that they could disintegrate with an inadvertent sneeze, each with an all-over design of spidery black writing on a black background, and each composed of a few larger pieces and a vast number of tiny fragments. The missing pieces – often in places of tantalizing significance – are as numerous as those that remain.

Even with the incomplete results available so far, these documents have begun to rewrite some of the hitherto shadowy story of Petra in the sixth century.[9] Not least among these revisions is a new view of an earthquake that occurred in the region on 9 July 551, previously assumed to have been so devastating that after it Petra virtually ceased to function. Yet it merits not a single mention in any of the documents; indeed, life continues on its generally smooth course, interrupted by the normal run of births, marriages, business deals, disputes, taxes and death. This unique archive, portraying three generations of an affluent land-owning Petra family, and some of their relatives by marriage, is known so far to span virtually the whole of the sixth century, and it may yet prove to include documents up to the time of the seventh-century fire. The archive includes dowry settlements, resolutions of disputes, sworn agreements to property divisions and exchanges, registrations of property sales, transfers of tax responsibilities and receipts for payments of civic and military taxes. Clearly Babatha, some 400 years earlier, was not the only person in the area who meticulously filed every document that might stand as evidence in legal cases. What other collections still lie undiscovered?

All the documents are in Greek,[10] in varying styles of handwriting and written by several different people whose spelling and grammar show a wide divergence in skill. Some writers explain their lumpish characters by saying that they are 'slow' or 'unpractised' in writing; one — surprisingly, a priest — hands over the writing to an associate 'because I lack precision, cannot write more, and am very slow, writing letter by letter'. Some documents were drawn up in a highly professional manner by a *symbolaiographos* — a cross between a scribe and a lawyer — using the official Greek language, but including Arabic words and names transliterated into Greek characters. A number of these Arabic place names survive in the Petra region today, giving a potent sense of the continuity of habitation in the area. While Greek was used for all legal and official purposes, we can assume that the writers' usual spoken language was Arabic; but it is completely unclear what script they were at home with — by the sixth century the Nabataean script had disappeared, and the few inscriptions from this period are in a very early form of Arabic.

A FRAGMENT OF ROLL 10 OF THE PETRA PAPYRI, ORIGINALLY 3.20 METRES LONG. IT DETAILS THE DIVISION OF EXTENSIVE PROPERTY BETWEEN THREE BROTHERS, BASSOS, EPIPHANIOS AND SABINOS, COUSINS OF THEODOROS, THE MAIN CHARACTER IN THE ARCHIVE. THIS FRAGMENT DESCRIBES PART OF EPIPHANIOS' SHARE, INCLUDING A 'DRY GARDEN' (I.E. NOT NEEDING IRRIGATION) AND SLAVES, AND THE OPENING LINES OF SABINOS' ALLOCATION, WITH SOME ARABIC PLACE-NAMES TRANSLITERATED INTO GREEK. PHOTO BY HENRY COWHERD/ROBERT E. MITTELSTAEDT; REPRODUCED BY COURTESY OF THE AMERICAN CENTER OF ORIENTAL RESEARCH, AMMAN.

The earliest dated document so far deciphered is from 513, while the latest is from 594; others, in which the date is lost or as yet unread, may well be either earlier or later than these. The main protagonist is Theodoros son of Obodianos, son of Obodianos, whose father's and grandfather's name proclaims their Nabataean origin. While Nabataean names have long been known to have survived up to this period in the Negev, this is the first time they are recorded in Petra itself. In 513 Obodianos son of Obodianos, so ill that he expected to die, drew up a will in which, apart from three gifts of money, he bequeathed 'all my belongings whatsoever which I leave behind', half to the 'Holy House [Monastery] of our Lord the Saint High Priest Aaron' (presumed to be that near the top of Jabal Haroun), and the other half to the 'most Holy Hospital of the Saint and Gloriously Triumphant Martyr Kyrikos' in Petra itself. He also charged his two executors to care for his mother Thaaious, providing her with food and clothing for as long as she lived. One of his executors was another Theodoros son of Obodianos — evidently not the main character of the archive, since he was not born until the following year, but very likely the brother of Obodianos son of Obodianos. This Theodoros was named in the document as archdeacon of the 'Church of our Blessed and All-Holy Lady, the Glorious God-bearing [*Theotokos*] and Ever-Virgin Mary'.

But Obodianos did not die then — indeed, it appears that he changed his will, because his son Theodoros inherited property from his father in 537, some 24 years later. Theodoros was then a deacon and he, too, later became archdeacon of the same church — presumably the one beside which the archive was found; and, since archdeacons are associated with episcopal churches, this may well have been the seat of the bishop of Petra. A Bishop Theodoros is mentioned in an undated document in the archive – very likely the one known from other sources as attending the anti-Monophysite Synod of Jerusalem in September 536, along with Eunomos, presbyter of the Petra church, and Anastasius, 'by the grace of God deacon and monk'. Petra had evidently remained orthodox – as the name of the church in the 513 document shows, no Nestorians here had stripped the Virgin of her *Theotokos* title; and Bishop Theodoros, at least, upheld the doctrine of the Dual Nature against Monophysitism.

Whatever doctrinal issues our deacon's superiors may have been tangling with, in 537 the important thing for the 23-year-old Theodoros (a minor under Byzantine law until the age of 25) may have been his marriage to Stephanous daughter of Patrophilos. Theodoros kept in his archive two documents that relate to all the minutiae of the marriage settlement which he had negotiated with his new father-in-law, who was also his maternal uncle. The first contract, drawn up at the time of the marriage, listed what was to become of the lands that Patrophilos had made over to Theodoros; it was a complex list, specifying all the possible variations in who should inherit depending on which family members might die first, and whether children as yet unborn might also be involved. As Theodoros was under age, a legal representative acted on his behalf. The second contract appears to have been worked out slowly and with much reflection, as was appropriate given the large sums of money involved. But it was amicably done and after two years – by which time Theodoros would have reached his majority – Stephanous' dowry property and bridal gifts were assessed at the equivalent value of nearly 3 kg of gold – about £12,500/$20,000 at today's prices.

In the same year that he was married, Theodoros set off for Gaza where he took part in the division of some family property – perhaps following the death of his father. There were several properties involved, each a considerable distance from the others, for they were at Gaza, Beersheba in the northern Negev and Eleutheropolis (Beith Guvrin) near Jerusalem. Over the following years Theodoros also acquired several plots of land in the Petra area – in 540, after complex negotiations over ownership and tax, he took over a vineyard at Beit Tell al-Keb; and four years later some land in Zadakatha (today's Sadaqa) was 'ceded' to him by his maternal great-uncle Dousarios son of Valens, whose name shows that this probably Christian man was named after the main Nabataean god.

The buying and selling of property and the settlement of property allocations and disputes figure considerably in Theodoros' documents – as presumably they did in his life. The ancient practice of defining a plot of land by its neighbours is, in these documents, the same as we saw it in the Babatha archive – first those to the east, then west, south and finally north. Area was still reckoned by how many *sata* and *kaboi* of grain could be sown, though by now the emphasis of these terms had shifted to refer more specifically to land measurement than to quantities of grain; and the Latin land measure, *iugerum*, was also used. Neither water rights nor legal rights were specified in the same detail, but the conditions attached to the agreement were spelled out at the conclusion of the document in a way that mirrors those of the Babatha archive, complete with catch-all phrases.

Some features are new – one being the greater emphasis put on the tax responsibility of the landowner. While before we saw land in the Roman census being assessed for the amount of tax due from it, here we see documents, quite separate from the bill of sale, dedicated to transferring the tax responsibility from the old owner to the new. Another novelty is that, in this now Christian empire, the parties no longer affirm their commitment by swearing 'by the Tyche of our lord the Emperor'; instead, they swear 'once and for all to one another the most horrifying oath by the Divine Holy Trinity and the Imperial Salvation'.

One fascinating document[11] shows how some disputes were settled in Petra, and perhaps other parts of the eastern Byzantine Empire. In 544 Theodoros brought charges against a fellow-deacon, Stephanos son of Leontios, his neighbour in Zadakatha. Instead of going to court, the case was heard by two leading men in the community – Theodoros son of Alpheios, 'the archdeacon of our most holy church' (and thus the superior of both litigants), and Thomas son of Boëthos, military prior at the army base at Zadakatha. These two arbitrators were charged 'to solve the case and bring it to completion in writing'. They took their duties seriously – their meticulous recording and resolution of the case took about 500 lines and 7 metres of papyrus scroll, of which several fragments are missing.

One of the disputed issues was that Stephanos had been taking rainwater from Theodoros' roof for his own use, but there was also a long list of grievances on both sides that had rankled between them and their fathers for several decades – indeed, a document cited as evidence in one issue was from 73 years earlier! It seems that there had been three previous attempts to resolve some of these disputes, but all had failed. Now every matter that was still at issue between the two men and their families was to be dealt with. Theodoros and Stephanos put their cases in writing; then both men made oral depositions in which the resentment that had festered between them could find unvarnished expression. Theodoros expostulated against Stephanos' unilateral appropriation of water from his roof, as well as all other perceived misdemeanours: 'If this were granted to whoever wished, then many men would be deprived of their lawful rights by the ill-doing of such people who wish — rather, who desire — to have other people's property in their possession.' Then, 'after much fighting', the arbitrators gave their judgements, item by item — Theodoros and Stephanos were both to have access to the rainwater collected from each other's roofs 'according to the old custom'; the open area of the dung store that they shared should have a wall put up, dividing the space according to a specified ratio, so that neither could gain access to the other's dung; and so on. If it was indeed an arbitration, all the judgements would have been binding on both parties.

Finally there were just two matters that could not be resolved in this way because they involved a misdemeanour that each believed the other had committed, but for which there was no proof — Theodoros believed that Stephanos had stolen timber, stone and even doors from his house; Stephanos believed that Theodoros had wronged his father, Leontios, over a payment following the sale of a vineyard. Both denied the charges, and both were required to affirm their innocence by a solemn oath taken on the Bible in the Holy Chapel of the Martyr St Kyrikos in Zadakatha. It was apparently inconceivable that either man would lie under such a holy oath — either he would affirm his innocence in all truth or he would admit his guilt and beg forgiveness; and such an apology would have to be accepted. In fact both swore their innocence, and the oaths had to be accepted as the end of the matter. The arbitration thus became a Nabataean-Byzantine type of Truth and Reconciliation Commission, a vital part of the healing process that was so badly needed between these two warring deacons.

In the Greek and Persian worlds arbitration is known from very ancient history and myth. Later, the Athenians created a precedent by appointing public arbitrators, men of maturity and experience, to settle disputes instead of them going to the civil courts; the Ptolemies adopted this idea in Egypt in the fourth century BC. The Romans, although largely uninfluenced by Greek legal practices, also occasionally resorted to arbitration. As for the Nabataeans, all we know of their legal proceedings is

Strabo's statement that in his day (around the turn of the first centuries BC/AD) only foreigners indulged in litigation, while the Nabataeans did not prosecute each other but 'in every way kept peace'. This can hardly mean that they had no disputes, but that they resolved them without recourse to the courts. In the Babatha archive, and other documents from the same area in the Roman provincial period, the only courts that are mentioned are those of the Roman governor; no local courts crop up at all, though this is no proof that they did not exist. Now, in the sixth century, we find the Hellenized Nabataeans in Petra involved in what appears to be an arbitration. It must be at least a possibility that they were following a long-established Nabataean tradition, based perhaps on earlier Greek practice, of resorting to arbitration rather than the courts to resolve whatever disputes they may have had.

Although Theodoros and his wife had a son, Panolbios, he appears to have died while still young. When Theodoros himself died around 592, his property and his papers were inherited by one or more of his relatives.

Petra appears to have continued in modest prosperity up to the time of the Islamic conquest. In southern Jordan this began in the years following 630, when the bishop of Aela (Aqaba) and leaders of Udhruh and Jarba (both near Petra), and of Maqna (on the coast south of Aela), made a peace treaty with the Prophet Mohammad at Tabuk in the northern Hejaz. Significantly the bishop of Petra was not among the peace-makers, probably because Petra was no longer the seat of the metropolitan bishop. We know from an inscription that in 687 there was a metropolitan bishop at Rabbath Moab; at some point before that — probably by 630, and perhaps even in the late sixth century — the see had been transferred from Petra to Rabbath Moab. The great church in Petra — terribly damaged by fire sometime in the seventh century — fell into disuse, and was later appropriated for squatter occupation.

Another collection of papyrus documents, found in 1935 at Nessana in the southern Negev, takes the story up to 689. Those from the Byzantine period show Arabic names written in Greek forms — already a common trend — but after the conquest we see a marked increase in names being expressed in their original Arabic forms. Land taxes, which had also figured in the Greek pre-conquest documents, were called *kharaj* in the Arabic documents of the Islamic period; and a new tax, *jiziya*, evolved into a kind of poll tax. All non-Muslims had to pay these taxes, but they were less onerous than those that had been imposed by the Byzantine authorities.

What was true for Nessana was true for the whole area: the resident population – mostly Christians, including the Nabataeans – could either choose to move out to places where life and trade were easier, or to stay where they were, cultivating their land and paying their taxes. Whether they chose to stay or to leave, their security was guaranteed; and the majority who stayed were assured freedom of worship and protection for their churches and all other property. Indeed new churches were built, and were decorated as the congregations wished. There was no compulsion to convert. At Sobata a mosque was built next to the south church, its design carefully adjusted so as not to damage the church, and Muslim and Christian forms of worship were performed side by side in apparent harmony.

In the Byzantine period the pressure of an expanding population had made the Negev a growth area, both in terms of population and agriculture. So now, with thousands of new settlers from Arabia to provide for, as well as the long-established residents, new settlements were established and new areas of land were put under cultivation throughout this and other southern areas of the erstwhile Nabataean lands.

As for Petra, doubtless many who could afford to leave took what money they had and moved on to more productive areas, either for agriculture or for trade. Wealthy families like that of Theodoros probably moved to their rich holdings at Zadakatha and other places outside the city, farming the land and paying their taxes. The least affluent would have had no option but to stay, squeezing as good a living as they could among the ruins and caves of the crumbling city. Probably they reverted to a semi-nomadic way of life, in autumn, winter and spring making the most of Petra's water sources and gardens, and in summer taking their flocks into the mountains to find pasture. Through these people and their descendants the ancient place names in the area would have been preserved. But as far as the outside world was concerned, a profound silence descended on the ancient capital of the Nabataeans.

Further to the north, in the lands that were still part of the Byzantine empire, the word 'Nabataean' quickly took on the increasingly pejorative meanings of 'peasant', 'boor' and 'bastard'. As an expression of ultimate contempt a man might be called a 'Nabataean son of a whore' – perhaps because the Byzantines believed that it was to the people of the old Nabataean lands that they owed their defeat at the hands of the Muslims. The competent but unpopular Byzantine Emperor Leo III (717–741), who came from the borders of the Byzantine Empire and the Arab lands, was referred to by his detractors as 'a Nabataean from Arabian Nabataea' – this once proud name had become the worst of insults. It was a tragic degradation for one of the ancient world's most gifted, magnificent and tolerant people.

EPILOGUE
The Nabataeans in the Islamic World

LONG BEFORE THE ISLAMIC CONQUEST OF SYRIA,[1] the Nabataeans had lost their social, cultural and religious identity. The process of social fragmentation may have begun in the last decades of the Nabataean kingdom, when some landowners in places like Mahoza sold their properties and moved elsewhere. Such resettlements continued in the Roman and Byzantine periods. Other Nabataeans may have reverted to a life of itinerant trade, though now dealing in different commodities, for there was no longer so rich a market for aromatics — early Christianity caused a temporary suspension of the use of incense in religious rituals, for it was too closely linked with pagan practice. Even when incense appeared in Christian worship in the late fourth century, the scale of its use was a shadow of its pagan past. In any case, it was now mainly transported by sea, bypassing the old overland routes. In the mid-sixth century, when Mecca's trade revived, many merchants (whose numbers would certainly have included some descendants of the Nabataeans) found new niches in the market, buying oil, wine and flour in the rich agricultural lands of Syria for sale in the arid and unproductive Hejaz.

WHEN CALIPH 'UMAR ENTERED JERUSALEM IN 638 HE DECLARED THE TEMPLE MOUNT, THEN A RUBBISH DUMP, TO BE A HOLY PRECINCT FOR ISLAM — THE HARAM ASH-SHARIF (NOBLE SANCTUARY). BUT IT WAS THE UMAYYAD CALIPH 'ABD AL-MALIK WHO BUILT THE MOSQUE, KNOWN AS THE DOME OF THE ROCK OR THE MOSQUE OF 'UMAR, AND DEDICATED IT IN 691 (PHOTO: SONIA HALLIDAY, SONIA HALLIDAY PHOTOGRAPHS).

Even among the majority of Nabataeans who remained part of the settled population in the province of Arabia, Roman and Byzantine rule had brought new social, cultural and religious divisions, particularly with the spread of Christianity and its profusion of heresies and schisms. Greek had replaced the Nabataean form of Aramaic as the language of official communication; and the widespread adoption of Greek or Roman names meant that many people were no longer distinguishable from any other ethnic group. The Nabataeans had not so much disappeared as baptized themselves out of recognition, becoming assimilated with the many other ethnic groups who inhabited the old Nabataean kingdom.

At least since the time of Alexander, the Nabataeans had spoken a form of Arabic while conducting all official business in another language — first Aramaic, more recently Greek and, under the Romans, some Latin too. Linguistically the Nabataeans were separate from their Roman rulers; culturally their common ground was only skin-deep. In religion, too, the intransigent imposition of orthodox Christian doctrine created splits within the Church from the fourth century onwards. And for the many Nabataeans (probably most) who became Christians, the language of their liturgy was neither Arabic nor Aramaic but the less familiar Greek. The Byzantine Empire was riven with divisions in every sphere.

To many Nabataeans the new Muslims of the Hejaz may have felt closer both ethnically and linguistically than their Byzantine masters — they were, after all, Arabs like themselves who spoke a recognizable, if somewhat different, form of Arabic. Even in religion, the Muslims' monotheism, their unity (at least to begin with), their use of Arabic in worship as in everyday life and their tolerance towards Christians may have given the Nabataeans a sense of fraternity rather than alienation. Better these Muslim brothers, they may have reasoned, than the divided Byzantines with whom they had no ties of blood and few of culture.

Arab and Muslim sources from the early centuries of Islam used the terms Anbat or Nabat to refer to some groups of people living in Syria or Mesopotamia. The words, meaning 'drawers of water', refer to settled agriculturalists, who lived in villages — peasants rather than rich land owners — to distinguish them from 'Arab' nomadic pastoralists. There is a temptation to translate the words as identifying ethnic Nabataeans, but in fact they have no such connotation — though some descendants of the Nabataeans were doubtless settled farmers and drawers of water, and some of them may have been included in the term.

In a late and somewhat dubious account, by 'Abd al-Mun'im al-Himyari, of the entry of Caliph 'Umar ibn al-Khattab (634-644) into Jerusalem, after the Muslims had captured the city in 638, we are told: 'When they had finished the writing of the treaty, they [the Greek patriarch of Jerusalem and his followers] opened the gate of Aelia to the Muslims, and 'Umar and his army entered. He compelled the Palestinian Nabataeans to sweep out the holy shrine, [now] the place of the Rock, for there was a great deal of rubbish.'[2] The Noble Sanctuary had been used as a rubbish dump during the Byzantine period but, so important was the place to Muslims, from its association with the Prophet Mohammad, that the Caliph himself joined in the work of cleansing it. According to al-Tabari (838-923), Caliph 'Umar 'stood up from his place of prayer and went to the rubbish ... He said, "Oh people, do what I am doing." He knelt in the midst of the rubbish and put it by the handful into the lower part of his mantle... By the time it was evening nothing remained of the rubbish.'[3] We cannot know the full story — but the image of this humble Caliph of Islam sharing such lowly toil with the humbled descendants of the Nabataeans is a moving one.

While most Nabataeans probably remained Christians at this stage, there are accounts of early conversions to Islam of 'Nabat', some of whom may have been Nabataeans. According to the tenth century writer al-Kufi, early in the caliphate of 'Umar ibn al-Khattab, the great Muslim general Abu 'Ubayda ibn al-Jarrah summoned a courier from the Syrian Nabat and told him:

"Look, when I give you this letter, run swiftly to reach the Commander of the Faithful, 'Umar ibn al-Khattab, and pass it on to him."... and the courier went off, running a harsh course, until he caught up with 'Umar ibn al-Khattab; when they conferred together the Caliph was astonished by [his] intelligence and perspicacity. He suggested that he become a Muslim — for the man was a Christian — and he did so, at the Caliph's hand.

There are no known references to Petra, after those in the sixth-century papyrus scrolls, until the early tenth century — for over 300 years the story of the city is almost a complete blank. But not quite. Recent excavations of tombs near the Ridge church have given clear evidence of tomb robbing — one a second-century AD Nabataean tomb that was robbed in the seventh or eighth century. Those Nabataeans who remained in the heart of Petra were probably, as we surmised earlier, from the eco-

THE ALMOST IMPREGNABLE AL-WU'EIRA CRUSADER CASTLE NEAR PETRA, BUILT BY KING BALDWIN I OF JERUSALEM IN 1115 TO DEFEND HIS EASTERN BORDER AGAINST SARACEN RAIDS.

nomically challenged stratum of society, with no option but to stay where they were and eke out as good an existence as they could in the poor circumstances they were faced with. There cannot have been more than 500 of them – all that the springs and the broken water installations could support. Many evidently became scavengers, selling whatever of value they could find to whoever would buy. An easy target was the great church – after the seventh-century fire it was systematically stripped of marble paving stones, and gold and glass tesserae from the broken wall and ceiling mosaics. From the old tombs the most interesting items would have been gold jewellery. Since archaeological excavations began in Petra in the early twentieth century, very few tombs have been found intact – the ancient scavengers had done a thorough job. Hopefully they had filled some hungry stomachs.

The Arab historian al-Mas'udi (died AD 928) broke the literary silence that had enveloped Petra with a reference to the area's highest peak, Jabal Haroun, as a holy mountain of the Christians. The monks there were more likely to have been descendants of Greek colonists than of the Nabataeans, and their liturgy would have been in Greek and of the Byzantine order. The next reference to Petra comes in the early twelfth century when Baldwin I, the Crusader king of Jerusalem, made his first raid into the lands east of the rift valley. According to Bishop Fulcher of Chartres, who accompanied the king, they found 'at the top of the mountain [Jabal Haroun] the Monastery of the holy Aaron where Moses and Aaron were wont to speak with God'.[5] The Greek Orthodox monks there felt under constant threat from Saracen raiders on the trade and communications route between Cairo and Damascus. And they clearly had a very different perspective from the local residents.

In 1107 the bedouin of the Petra/Wadi Mousa area – quite possibly descended from the scavengers – invited Toghtekin, the Turkish ruler of Damascus, to send a force to Petra to establish a base from which raiding parties could be sent against the Crusaders in Palestine. It is possible that they did this because they shared the Turks' Islamic faith, but this is sheer speculation. When the monks asked Baldwin to intervene, he brought a force of 500 knights and marched close to the Turkish camp; he also spread rumours that a large army was on its way. Believing the rumours, the Turks rapidly decamped back to Damascus. To punish the bedouin who had invited the Turks, Baldwin smoked them out of the caves in which they lived and carried off their flocks. According to Albert of Aix,[6] when the Crusaders returned to Jerusalem, many of the local Christians (also quite possibly descendants of the Nabataeans) went with them, for they feared reprisals from the bedouin.

Thirty-seven years later it may again have been the inhabitants of Petra/Wadi Mousa who invited the Turks to return, this time to besiege the castle that the Crusaders had built in 1115 in an almost impregnable position near the ancient ruins. William of Tyre[7] wrote that the Turks succeeded in occupying the castle, but when the Crusaders started to root out and burn the 'luxuriant olive groves… [from which] the inhabitants of the land made their living… as their fathers had done before them', the local people quickly reconsidered their position. They agreed to surrender the castle provided the Turks could withdraw unharmed, and they themselves would not be punished. The Crusaders held the castle until 1189 – it was the last stronghold east of the rift valley to surrender to Salah ad-Din (Saladin). When the Christian pilgrim Thetmar visited in 1217 he found Petra uninhabited, and only two Greek monks were still living in lonely isolation in the monastery on Jabal Haroun. Nearly 60 years later, in 1276, when the Mamluk Sultan Baibars passed through Petra on his way from Cairo to Kerak,[8] there is no mention of people living in the ancient capital of the Nabataeans.

In the interval between Baibars' visit and that of Johann Ludwig Burckhardt in 1812 Petra appears to have dropped out of western minds and maps. The fact that both Thetmar and Baibars (and also Burckhardt) found no one living in the ancient site at the seasons they went there does not necessarily mean there were none at other seasons. Baibars came in early June, Burckhardt in mid-August – times when the bedouin were likely to be high in the mountains with their flocks, seeking whatever pasture was available in these dry months. Yet Burckhardt's guide

JOHANN LUDWIG BURCKHARDT, WHO IN 1812 BECAME THE FIRST KNOWN WESTERNER TO SEE PETRA SINCE THE CHRISTIAN PILGRIM THETMAR IN 1217.

themselves to be distinguished from all later intruders, whether Greek, Roman or Arab.

The origin of the tribe's name has also given rise to speculation. It is widely accepted that it comes from the Arabic *badala* (change). In 1929 Dr Tawfik Canaan, while recording folk tales and place names in Petra, was told a story of the origin of the Bdoul by members of the neighbouring Liyathna tribe, who were not noted for their friendliness to the bedouin:

> When Moses and the Israelites surrounded Petra he [Moses] declared war against the inhabitants and conquered and slaughtered them all except twelve who hid themselves in a cave on the top of the mountain *Umm el-Biyârah*. Moses ordered them to come down. They answered '*innâ abdalnâ yâ nabiy allâh*.' We have changed, O prophet of God. 'What have you changed?' asked Moses. 'Our religion; for we accept yours,' was the answer. Since that time they are known as *Bdul*. How much of this legend can be accepted as true and pointing to their possible origin from the old Nabataeans it is impossible to say.[9]

Hardly surprisingly, the Bdoul did not accept this explanation. Indeed the Bdoul themselves told people (a few still do) that their name, with its meaning of 'change', came because the ancient inhabitants of Petra, their ancestors, changed their religion from Judaism to Christianity, and later to Islam — as some Christian Nabataeans undoubtedly did. Other members of the Bdoul eliminated all references to a change in religion and claimed that their name came from Badl, son of an otherwise unknown Nabataean king called Nabṭ — a neat, if fanciful, explanation which includes a claim to descent from the Nabataean people with whom Petra is so inextricably identified.

That the Nabataeans might be ancestors of the Bdoul must at least be a possibility, though impossible to prove with the present state of knowledge. There is no known connection between the scavengers of the eighth century and the cave-dwelling bedouin who opposed the Crusaders in the twelfth century, nor between these bedouin and the Bdoul whom western travellers first encountered (also living in the caves of Petra) in the early nineteenth century. Only if DNA samples could be taken from skeletons found in an undeniably Nabataean context, and if a close match were found in a living person, could a connection be proved. If such a match were found the mystery of the fate of the Nabataeans would have at least a partial solution; if not, the mystery remains.

(from the Liyathna tribe of Wadi Mousa village, but originally from Kerak) was in constant fear that they might be seen — presumably by the bedouin of the area who would not welcome such intrusion into their territory. These bedouin may well have been the Bdoul tribe for only six years later, when Commanders Irby and Mangles came here, they found the whole of Petra controlled by the Bdoul under their charismatic and awe-inspiring sheikh, Imqaibal Abu Zeitun, 'father of olives'. They were clearly not newcomers in the region. Today they are the oldest known inhabitants of Petra.

In the nineteenth century those western travellers who were able to communicate in a friendly manner with the Bdoul learned from them that they believed they were descended from the 'Bene Israel', sons of Israel, the most ancient inhabitants of the area who had first carved the monuments of Petra that were now their homes — a bizarre conflation of the Israelites of Moses with the Nabataeans. In any case they clearly considered

❧ NOTES ❧

PRELUDE

1 Both stories are found in Plutarch's charming, if unreliable *Life of Alexander*, 25, 6.

Chapter I

1 David Graf, 'The Origin of the Nabateans,' *Aram*, 2, 1990, 45–75.

2 Genesis 25: 13; 28: 9; 36: 7; Isaiah 60:7.

3 Diodorus, II, 48, 1; XIX, 94, 2–4, 9–10.

4 Diodorus, XIX, 94, 6–8.

5 Diodorus, XIX, 94, 5.

6 Herodotus, *Histories*, IV, 44.

7 Herodotus, *Histories*, III, 108.

8 Harold Ingrams's Burton Memorial Lecture, 'From Cana (Husn al-Ghorab) to Sabbatha (Shabwa): The South Arabian Incense Road,' *Journal of the Royal Asiatic Society*, 1945, Parts 3 & 4, 169–185.

9 All Theophrastus quotations are from IX, 4, 1–10.

10 Fawzi Zayadine, 'Cosmetic Techniques: A Historical and Botanical Approach,' *Studies in the History and Archaeology of Jordan*, 5, Amman, 1995, 67–75.

11 Pliny, *Natural History*, XII, 32, 63–65

CHAPTER 2

1 Diodorus, XIX, 95-97.

2 Fawzi Zayadine, 'Un relief néo-babylonien à Sela près de Talifeh: Interprétation Historique,' *Syria* 76, 1999, 83–90.

3 By Dr Hamed Qatamin of Mu'tah University, Jordan.

4 2 Samuel 8: 13–14.

5 1 Kings 11: 16.

6 Ezekiel 35: 5; 36: 5.

7 Isaiah 34: 5–13, Authorised Version. The New Revised Standard Version more prosaically (and accurately) gives us 'jackals' instead of 'dragons'.

8 Diodorus, XIX, 98–100.

9 David Graf, 'The Origin of the Nabataeans', *Aram*, 2, 1990, 45–75.

10 J. Starcky, 'Les inscriptions nabatéennes et l'histoire de la Syrie méridionale et du Nord de la Jordanie', in J.-M. Dentzer (ed.), *Hauran*, Part I, Paris, 1985, 167–168.

11 2 Maccabees 5: 8 (Apocrypha).

12 Josephus, *The Antiquities of the Jews*, XII, 8, 3.

13 Josephus, *ibid.*, XIII, I, 2.

14 David Graf, 'The Roman East from the Chinese Perspective', in *Annales Archéologiques Arabes-Syriennes*, 42, 1996, 199–216.

CHAPTER 3

1 Josephus, *The Wars of the Jews*, I, 4, 6.

2 The Romanized form of Judah.

3 In Justin's *Epitome* of Pompeius Trogus, 39, 5, the king to whom he gives the Hellenized name Herotimus is believed to refer to Aretas II.

4 I am indebted to Dr Fawzi Zayadine for this translation.

5 In Uranios' *Arabika*, quoted in John Oleson, 'Humeima Hydraulic Survey, 1989', *Echos du Monde Classique/Classical Views*, 34, n.s. 9, 1990, 145–163.

6 Ten years later he was tried in Rome on a charge of extortion during his governorship in Sardinia.

CHAPTER 4

1 Josephus, *The Antiquities of the Jews*, XVI, 7, 6.

2 Strabo, *Geography*, XVI, 4.

3 G.W. Bowersock, 'Perfumes and Power,' in *Profumi d'Arabia*, *Atti del convegno a cura di Alessandra Avanzini*, Rome, 1997, 543–556.

4 An inscription commissioned by Syllaeus at Miletus describes him as 'brother of the king', i.e. Obodas III. It also refers to him as 'son of Teimu'; if he had been a blood-brother, he would have been named as 'son of Malichus the king, king of the Nabataeans'.

5 Syllaeus is known to have minted his own coins; though undated, they may come from the period shortly before Obodas III's death.

6 G.W. Bowersock, 'Nabataeans on the Capitoline,' *Hyperboreus*, 3, 1997, Fasc. 2, 347–352.

7 Tacitus, *Annals*, II, 57.

8 Professor G.W. Bowersock, in a personal communication, points out that Aretas would only have entertained Roman officials inside his own kingdom; he suggests that Damascus may have been back in Nabataean hands some years earlier than is generally assumed, in which case the banquet could have been held there.

9 Matthew 14: 3–11; Mark 6: 17-29; Luke 3: 18–21.

10 It was also the place of John the Baptist's imprisonment and execution.

11 2 Corinthians 11:32–33.

12 Dio's *Roman History*, LIII, 30, 5.

CHAPTER 5

1 The most authoritative and comprehensive study is Judith McKenzie's *The Architecture of Petra*, Oxford, 1990.

2 Thought to be the more strictly Nabataean form of the name Malichus.

3 I Maccabees 13: 27–29.

4 The -t at the end of Khaznet in 'Khaznet Far'oun' disappears when the word is used in isolation. It thus becomes Khazne(h).

5 Another was found in the kiln that was discovered in Wadi Mousa town.

6 'Basilica' comes from the Greek *basilike oikia*, king's house (king = *basileus*).

7 Rolf A. Stucky, 'The Nabataean House and the Urbanistic System of the Habitation Quarters in Petra', *Studies in the History and Archaeology of Jordan* 5, Amman, 1995, 193-198.

CHAPTER 6

1 Genesis 28:22.

2 R. N. Jones *et al.*, 'A Second Nabataean Inscription from Tell esh-Shuqafiya, Egypt', *Bulletin of the American Schools of Oriental Research*, 269, 1988, 47–57.

3 John Healey, 'Dushara as Sun-god', in *I Primi Sessanta Anni di Scuola: Studi dedicati dagli amici a Sergio Noja Noseda ne suo 65° compleanno*, 7 July 1996, 37–53.

4 See G. W. Bowersock, 'The Cult and Representation of Dusares in Roman Arabia', in Fawzi Zayadine (ed.), *Petra and the Caravan Cities*, Amman, 1990, 31-33.

5 Ernst Axel Knauf, 'Dushara and Shai' al-Qaum', *Aram*, 2, 1990, 175-183.

6 Pau Figueras, 'The Roman Worship of Athena-Allat in the Decapolis and the Negev', *Aram*, 4, 1992, 173–183.

7 See Fawzi Zayadine's article on Manat (Manawat) in *Lexicon Iconographicum Mythologiae Classicae*, Vol. VIII (Supp.), 805–806.

8 Z. al-Muheisen & F. Villeneuve, 'Fifteen Years of Archaeological Research at Khirbet edh-Dharih', *Studies in the History and Archaeology of Jordan*, 7, Amman, forthcoming.

CHAPTER 7

1 Richard Pococke, *A Description of the East and some other Countries*, vol. 1, London, 1743.

2 Robert Clayton (trans.), *A Journal from Grand Cairo to Mount Sinai and Back Again*, London, 1753.

3 Carsten Niebuhr, *Travels in Arabia and other Countries in the East*, Edinburgh, 1792.

4 J. L. Burckhardt, *Travels in Syria and the Holy Land*, London, 1822; reprinted New York, 1983.

5 Charles Forster, *The One Primeval Language*, London, 1851.

6 J. Naveh, 'A Nabatean Incantation Text', *Israel Exploration Journal*, 29, No. 2, 1979, 111–119.

7 It was not until 1900–11 that the Hejaz Railway

was built from Damascus to Madina, with an important provisioning station at Meda'in Saleh; its stated purpose was to facilitate the Haj pilgrimage.

8 Charles Doughty, *Travels in Arabia Deserta*, London, 1888.

9 Now in the Istanbul Archaeological Museum.

10 An alternative interpretation proposes not a deity called Qaysha but an object, *qaysa*, the measuring rod of the goddess Manat.

11 E. H. Palmer, *The Desert of Exodus*, 2 vols., London, 1871.

12 In Islamic tradition it was not Isaac, but Abraham's older son Ishmael, by the Egyptian maid Hagar, who was to be sacrificed.

13 From Zebed in northern Syria (AD 512); Harran in south-east Turkey (AD 568); and Umm al-Jimal in northern Jordan (undated, but evidently sixth century).

CHAPTER 8

1 Werner Eck, 'The Bar Kokhba Revolt: The Roman Point of View', *Journal of Roman Studies*, 89, 1999, 76–89.

2 Some bedouin discovered the cave several years earlier; one document they found, possibly from the Babatha archive, was published by J. Starcky in *Revue Biblique*, 61, 1954, 161–181.

3 Yigael Yadin, Jonas C. Greenfield, Ada Yardeni and Baruch Levine, *Hebrew, Aramaic and Nabataean Documents from the Cave of Letters*, Jerusalem, forthcoming. It is the companion volume to Naphtali Lewis, *The Documents from the Bar Kokhba Period in the Cave of Letters: Greek Papyri*, Jerusalem, 1989.

4 Hannah M. Cotton and Jonas C. Greenfield, 'Babatha's *Patria*: Mahoza, Mahoz 'Eglatain and Zo'ar', *Zeitschrift für Papyrologie und Epigraphik*, 107, 1995, 126–134.

5 Hannah M. Cotton, 'The Languages of the Legal and Administrative Documents from the Judaean Desert', *Zeitschrift für Papyrologie und Epigraphik*, 125, 1999, 219–231.

6 An uncertain term, perhaps referring to coins minted in the last years of the Nabataean kingdom which, being of low silver content, would have turned black easily; they were not fully replaced by Trajan's coins.

7 Hannah M. Cotton, 'Deeds of Gift and the Law of Succession in the Documents from the Judaean Desert', *Akten des 21. Internationalen Papyrologenkongresses, Berlin, 1995, Archiv für Papyrusforschung*, Supplement 3, 1997, 179–186.

8 Hannah M. Cotton, 'The Guardianship of Jesus son of Babatha: Roman and Local Law in the Province of Arabia', *Journal of Roman Studies*, 83, 1993, 94–108.

9 Hannah M. Cotton, 'The Guardian (ЕПІТРОПОС) of a Woman in the Documents from the Judaean Desert', *Zeitschrift für Papyrologie und Epigraphik*, 118, 1997, 267–273.

10 Yigael Yadin, Jonas C. Greenfield and Ada Yardeni, 'Babatha's *Ketubba*', *Israel Exploration Journal*, 44, 1–2, 1994, 75–99.

11 Little over a year later Sextius Florentinus was dead; he was buried at his own request in an elaborately carved tomb in Petra. It was these references in the Babatha archive that enabled the tomb to be dated.

12 This peripatetic administration of justice seems to be referred to in a Chinese description of 'Li-kan' (thought to be identified with Reqem, the early Semitic name for Petra and its kingdom). Known as the *Hou-han-shu*, the document relates to the period AD 25–220 – both before and after the Roman annexation of Nabataea. As the Nabataean kings are not known to have held assizes in different parts of their kingdom, this must describe the practice of the Roman governors. But it is no eye-witness account; rather it is an amalgam of several imperfectly understood responses by visitors from 'Li-kan' to the Chinese court, or traders who were questioned in foreign ports. It states: 'In the city there are five palaces... The king goes to one palace a day to hear cases. After five days he has completed his round. As a rule, they let a man with a bag follow the king's carriage. Those who have some matter to submit, throw a petition into the bag. When the king arrives at the palace, he examines into the rights and wrongs of the matter.' It is easy enough to imagine the word for 'province' being mistranslated into Chinese as 'city', 'governor' as 'king', and 'month' being mistaken for 'day'. See F. Hirth's *China and the Roman Orient*, Leipzig, 1885.

CHAPTER 9

1 Aelius Aristides, *Panegyric to Rome* (Orations 26, 70, 100) ed. B. Keil, Berlin, 1898.

2 This, and several other references to Christians in Petra, I owe to Robert Schick's essay, 'The Ecclesiastical History of Petra', in Zbigniew T. Fiema *et al.*, *The Petra Church Project*, American Center of Oriental Research Publication No. 3, Amman, in press.

3 J.-P. Migne (ed.), *Patrologia Latina*, 23, Paris, 1878, col. 41f.

4 The name of the town is evocatively similar to that of Venus-Aphrodite's Nabataean counterpart, al-'Uzza.

5 *The Panarion of St Epiphanius, Bishop of Salamis*, trans. Philip R. Amidon SJ, New York and Oxford, 1990.

6 François Nau, 'Deux Episodes de l'histoire juive sous Théodose II (423 et 438) d'après la vie de Barsauma le Syrien', *Revue des Etudes Juives*, 83, 1927, 184–206.

7 John of Ephesus, *Lives of the Eastern Saints*, Part I, ed. and trans. by E. W. Brooks, in *Patrologia Orientalis*, Vol. 17, 1923, 1–306.

8 They have been conserved by a team of Finnish papyrologists led by Dr Jaakko Frösén of the Finnish Academy and the University of Helsinki, and are currently being deciphered by two teams – that of Dr Frösén, and one from the University of Michigan headed by Dr Ludwig Koenen. Publication should begin in 2001.

9 Jaakko Frösén, 'The First Five Years of the Petra Papyri', *Atti del XXII Congresso Internazionale di Papyrologia*, (Firenze, 23–29 agosto 1998), Florence, forthcoming; Ludwig Koenen, 'Petra in the Sixth Century: The Carbonized Papyri', in Glenn Markoe (ed.), Nabataean volume in preparation.

10 A few lines in one document are in Latin.

11 Maarit Kaimio, 'P. Petra inv. 83: A Settlement of Dispute', *Atti del XXII Congresso Internazionale di Papirologia*, (Firenze, 23–29 agosto 1998), Florence, forthcoming.

EPILOGUE

1 The term includes present-day Syria, Jordan, Israel and Palestine.

2 Quoted from Salih Hamarneh, 'The Nabataeans after the Decline of their Political Power: From the Arabic Islamic Sources', *Aram*, 2, 1990, 425–436.

3 Ibn A'tham Ahmad al-Kufi, *Kitab al-Futuh*, Vol. I, 187–189.

4 Zbigniew T. Fiema *et al.*, *The Petra Church Project*, American Center of Oriental Research Publication No. 3, Amman, in press.

5 Fulcher of Chartres, *A History of the Expedition to Jerusalem*, trans. Frances Rita Ryan, Knoxville, 1969.

6 Albert of Aix, *Historiae*, in *Recueil des Historiens des Croisades – Historiens Occidentaux*, Vol. 4, Paris, 1879.

7 William of Tyre, *A History of Deeds Done beyond the Sea*, trans. E. A. Babcock and A. C. Krey, New York, 1976.

8 Fawzi Zayadine, 'Caravan Routes Between Egypt and Nabataea and the Voyage of Sultan Baibars to Petra in 1276', *Studies in the History and Archaeology of Jordan*, 2, Amman, 1985, 159–174.

9 Tawfik Canaan, 'Studies in the Topography and Folklore of Petra', *Journal of the Palestine Oriental Society* 9, 3-4, 1929, 136–218

GLOSSARY

ACANTHUS A common Mediterranean prickly plant whose spiny leaves inspired some Greek decorative ideas, particularly on the Corinthian capital.

ACROTERION (Greek; pl. acroteria) The ornament at the apex and lower angles of a pediment, usually on a plinth.

AGORA A public square or market-place in a Greek or Hellenistic city, corresponding to the Roman forum.

AMBULATORY A space for walking in, in particular around the outer areas of the interior of a church or temple.

ANICONIC Without imagery, especially of the human form (Greek *an* = without + *eikon* = image).

ANTHROPOMORPHIC In human form (Greek *anthropos* = human being + *morphe* = form).

APSE A semicircular recess, often vaulted, either in a wall or at the end of a building.

ARCHITRAVE A stone lintel or wooden beam reaching from the top of one column or pier to another; the lowest section of an entablature.

ASHLAR MASONRY Masonry of squared stone set in regular horizontal courses, and with vertical joints.

ATRIUM The entrance courtyard to a Roman house or a Byzantine church, often with a roofed colonnade around the sides.

BARREL VAULT The roof of a room in the shape of a continuous arch.

BASILICA (Greek; from *basilike oikia* = house of the king) A rectangular building with two rows of columns in the longitudinal axis, and often with a recess in one side. In Roman times it was used as a law court, meeting hall or exchange. Since it had no associations with pagan religion, it was adopted for church architecture in the Byzantine period.

BOULEUTERION The building for meetings of the council (*boule*) of a Greek town.

BROKEN PEDIMENT A decorative architectural feature in the form of two half-pediments with a recess or a blank space between them.

CAPITAL The decorated topmost element of a column.

CAVEA The auditorium of a theatre, so named because early theatres were excavated from a hillside.

CAVETTO A concave moulding, usually a quarter-circle.

CELLA (Latin) The principal enclosed chamber or sanctuary of a temple.

COLONNADE A row of columns.

CORINTHIAN A type of capital decorated with volutes and acanthus leaves, invented (supposedly at Corinth) as a substitute for the Ionic order.

CORNICE The crowning and projecting section of the entablature; it is also used for any projection on a wall, designed to direct rainwater off the face of the building.

CROWSTEPS A pyramidal stepped design used as decoration on Nabataean tombs, either in a narrow horizontal band of multiple crowsteps or in a single monumental pair of steps over a cavetto cornice; also called 'Assyrian crowsteps' from the use of this design in Assyrian architecture.

DORIC An order evolved in the Dorian and western regions of Greece, based on a capital with minimal decoration.

DORIC FRIEZE A frieze of triglyphs and metopes.

DRUM A cylindrical section of a column; Nabataean column drums, in places (like Petra) where the material was soft sandstone, were much shorter than those of classical columns.

ENGAGED COLUMN A semidetached column, usually semicircular in plan, projecting from a wall.

ENTABLATURE The horizontal superstructure connecting a row of columns; or, sometimes, used to complete the architectural harmony of a wall. It is usually divided into three parts: supporting architrave, decorative frieze, projecting cornice.

EXEDRA (Latin; pl. exedrae) A recess, usually semicircular.

FRIEZE The middle section of an entablature, usually decorated.

HIPPODAMIAN GRID The concept of town planning developed by Hippodamus of Miletus in the fifth century BC, based on a grid of rectangular segments.

JABAL (Arabic; pl. *jibaal*) Mountain.

KHIRBE(T) (Arabic) Ruin.

LINTEL The horizontal beam over a door or window, or spanning the gap between two columns or piers.

METOPE (Greek = between the holes) The circular parts of a Doric frieze between the triglyphs; they could be carved or left plain.

NAVE The central aisle of a basilica between the colonnades and side aisles.

NECROPOLIS (Greek; from *nekros* = corpse and *polis* = city). The burial ground, or city of the dead, outside a Greek city.

NEFESH A Semitic word meaning 'breath' or 'spirit' which was used to refer to a memorial stele; the Nabataeans represented the dead person in pyramidal or conical form.

NIKE (Greek; pl. Nikai) The personification of Victory, represented with wings.

NYMPHAEUM Originally a temple of the nymphs; it became a public fountain house, usually decorated with statues of nymphs.

ODEON A roofed building containing a small theatre for musical performances or competitions.

OPUS SECTILE A type of mosaic pavement executed with pieces of coloured marble or stone, larger than traditional tesserae, in a geometrical or stylized floral pattern.

ORCHESTRA (Greek; from *orkheomai* = to dance) Originally the dancing place for the chorus in a Greek theatre, between the cavea and the stage; usually circular in a Greek theatre and semicircular in a Roman theatre.

ORDER The architectural system composed of column and entablature together.

PEDIMENT Originally the triangular element crowning the portico of a building; pediments are also used above niches, doors or bays, in varying shapes – triangular, segmental (arched) and broken.

PERIPTERAL A design of temple in which the cella is surrounded by a peristyle.

PERISTYLE A covered colonnade which either surrounds a peripteral building, or runs around an internal courtyard.

PIER A solid rectangular masonry support, usually free-standing but sometimes engaged; like columns, carrying an entablature or arch.

PILASTER A slender engaged pier with no structural function.

PODIUM A low wall or continuous pedestal on which columns or entire temples are carried.

PORTICO A colonnade, or a colonnaded entrance to a building.

STELE (Greek; pl stelae) An upright stone slab with sculptured reliefs or inscription, often used as a tombstone.

STUCCO The thin lime facing applied to brick or plaster for protection.

TEMENOS The sacred precinct of a temple, where worshippers gathered.

THOLOS A Greek circular building usually surrounded by columns.

TRICLINIUM (Latin; from *tri* = three, and *clinium* = benches; pl. triclinia) A dining room with benches

around three sides. With the Nabataeans the room was a chamber cut into the rock, with rock-cut benches, and the feasts were usually in memory of a dead person.

TRIGLYPH The panel in a Doric frieze between circular metopes, consisting of three vertical blocks like miniature pilasters, separated by grooves.

VAULT The roof of a room or part of a building which, in a variety of forms, is based on the principle of the arch.

VOLUTE The spiral scroll at each corner of a capital.

WADI (Arabic) A valley or watercourse, dry except during rain.

❧ CHRONOLOGY ❧

THE NABATAEAN KINGS

*c.*168 BC	Aretas I
? late 2nd C BC	Rabbel I
*c.*103–96 BC	Aretas II
*c.*96–86 BC	Obodas I
86–62 BC	Aretas III, 'Philhellene'
62–59 BC	Obodas II
59–30 BC	Malichus I
30–9 BC	Obodas III
9 BC–AD 40	Aretas IV, 'who loves his people'
AD 40–70	Malichus II
AD 70–106	Rabbel II, 'who brings life and deliverance to his people'

BEFORE THE KINGDOM

333 BC Alexander the Great defeats the Persians at the Battle of Issus

332 BC Alexander the Great captures Gaza

323 BC Death of Alexander the Great

*c.*312 BC Army of Antigonus the One-Eyed attacks Nabataean stronghold

259 BC Envoys of Ptolemy II meet Nabataeans in southern Syria

late 3rd C BC Ptolemaic fleet punishes Nabataean 'pirates' in Red Sea

ARETAS I *c.*168 BC

1st half 2nd C BC Inscription in Elusa, Negev, mentions 'Aretas, king of the Nabataeans'

*c.*168 BC Jason, ex-high priest of the Jews flees to 'Aretas, ruler of the Nabataeans'

167 BC Maccabean revolt against Antiochus IV of Syria

*c.*163 BC Judas Maccabeus meets Nabataeans 'peaceably'

RABBEL I Late second century BC

late 2nd C BC ?? first Nabataean coins minted

129 BC Moschion of Priene visits Petra on diplomatic tour of eastern Mediterranean

ARETAS II *c.*103–96 BC (relationship to previous kings unknown)

100 BC Birth of Julius Caesar

*c.*100 BC Gaza asks Aretas II for help against attack by Alexander Jannaeus of Judaea

OBODAS I *c.*96–86 BC (son of Aretas II)

*c.*93 BC Obodas I defeats Judaeans under Alexander Jannaeus

87 BC Obodas I defeats Seleucids of Syria under Antiochus XII

ARETAS III, 'PHILHELLENE' 86–62 BC (son of Obodas I)

? c.85 BC al-Khazneh (Treasury) carved in Petra by Alexandrian craftsmen

85–71 BC Aretas III adds Damascus to Nabataean kingdom

82 BC Aretas III defeats Alexander Jannaeus inside Judaea

76 BC Death of Alexander Jannaeus; succession of wife Salome Alexandra

67 BC Death of Salome Alexandra; son Hyrcanus succeeds in Judaea

65 BC Herod (the Great), as a child, given refuge in Petra

64 BC Pompey annexes Seleucid kingdom and creates Roman province of Syria

63 BC Pompey's expedition against Petra aborted

63 BC Birth of Gaius Octavius (Octavian), future Emperor Augustus

OBODAS II 62–59 BC (relationship to Aretas III unknown)

60 BC Julius Caesar elected consul in Rome

MALICHUS I 59–30 BC (relationship to Obodas II unknown)

55 BC Gabinius, Roman governor of Syria, defeats Nabataeans

49–31 BC Roman civil wars (first between Pompey and Julius Caesar)

47 BC Nabataeans send forces to Julius Caesar; Cleopatra Queen of Egypt

44 BC Julius Caesar murdered by conspirators led by Brutus and Cassius

43 BC London founded

42 BC Mark Antony and Octavian defeat Brutus and Cassius at Philippi

40 BC Roman general Labienus and Parthian allies capture Jerusalem/Herod seeks help from Malichus I in Petra; then goes to Rome

37 BC Romans appoint Herod King of Judaea/Parthians driven from Jerusalem/Cleopatra asks Antony for Judaea and Nabataea – request refused

31 BC Herod and Malichus I go to war (Nabataeans defeated)/ Octavian defeats Mark Antony at Battle of Actium

30 BC Malichus I burns Cleopatra's fleet/suicide of Cleopatra/ Octavian annexes Egypt

OBODAS III 30–9 BC (relationship to Malichus I unknown)

27 BC Octavian named Caesar Augustus by Senate

26–25 BC Augustus sends Roman army, including 1000 Nabataeans, to Arabia

late 1st C BC Building of Qasr al-Bint and Great temple in Petra

c.12 BC Syllaeus, Nabataean chief minister, proposes marriage to Herod's sister

9 BC Syllaeus goes to Rome to complain about Herod/death of Obodas III

ARETAS IV, 'WHO LOVES HIS PEOPLE' 9 BC–AD 40 (possibly descended from Malichus I)

9 BC Syllaeus seeks Augustus' support for own accession to Nabataean throne/Aretas IV accuses Syllaeus of poisoning Obodas III

6 BC Syllaeus, back in East, plots to murder Herod/flees to Rome/ executed

? 6 BC Birth of Jesus of Nazareth

4 BC Death of Herod the Great; kingdom divided between three sons/Aretas IV helps Romans put down popular Jewish revolt

early 1st C BC Development of Hegra in south of kingdom

early 1st C BC Carving of theatre in Petra

AD 14 Death of Augustus; accession of Emperor Tiberius

AD 27 Herod Antipas, tetrarch of Galilee and Peraea, divorces Nabataean wife

? AD 28 Death of John the Baptist

? AD 30 Death of Jesus of Nazareth

AD 37 Death of Tiberius; accession of Caligula

MALICHUS II AD 40–70 (son of Aretas IV)

AD 41 Death of Caligula; accession of Claudius

AD 54 Death of Claudius; accession of Nero

AD 60 Death of Nero; accession of Galba

mid–1st C AD Carving of ad-Deir (Monastery) in Petra

AD 66–74 First Jewish Revolt against Romans

AD 68 Flavius Josephus, *History of the Jewish War*

AD 69 The year of the 3 Emperors – Otho, Vitellius, Vespasian

AD 70 Roman destruction of Jerusalem and temple, with help from Malichus II

RABBEL II, 'WHO BRINGS LIFE AND DELIVERANCE TO HIS PEOPLE' AD 70–106 (son of Malichus II)

AD 79 Death of Vespasian; accession of Titus

AD 81 Death of Titus; accession of Domitian

AD 96 Death of Domitian; accession of Nerva

AD 98 Death of Nerva; accession of Trajan

AD 106 Emperor Trajan annexes Nabataea and creates province of Arabia

AFTER THE KINGDOM

AD 111–114 Trajan's new road (Via Nova Traiana) built: Bostra-Petra-Aela (Aqaba)

AD 113/4 Earthquake causes damage in Petra

AD 115 Death of Trajan; accession of Hadrian

c.AD 129 Roman governor Sextius Florentinus buried in a carved tomb in Petra

AD 130 Hadrian names Petra after himself – *Hadriane Petra*

AD 132–135 Second Jewish Revolt against Roman rule

AD 244–249 Philip, the first Arab Roman Emperor

AD 247 Actia Dusaria games held in Bostra to celebrate Rome's 1000th anniversary

AD 284–305 Emperor Diocletian; persecution of Christians (including at Petra)

AD 306–337 Emperor Constantine the Great; Christianity legalised

AD 330 Constantinople becomes new capital of Roman Empire

AD 363 Earthquake causes much damage in Petra

late 4th/early 5th C AD Ridge church built in Petra

AD 423 Barsauma and a gang of 40 monks convert pagan priests at Petra

AD 446 Urn tomb in Petra converted into a church

AD 570 Birth of Prophet Mohammed

AD 630 Beginning of Muslim conquest of eastern Byzantine Empire

AD 632 Death of Prophet Mohammed

AD 661–750 Umayyad Caliphate, first dynasty of Islam

AD 1099 Crusaders capture Jerusalem

AD 1100 Crusaders' first visit to Petra

SELECT BIBLIOGRAPHY

Articles and journals are referred to in footnotes in the text.

CLASSICAL AUTHORS

AGARTHARKIDES OF CNIDUS, in Anon., *Periplus of the Erythraean Sea.*

ANON., *Periplus of the Erythraean Sea*, trans. & ed. G. W. B. Huntingford, London, 1980.

Dio's Roman History, 9 vols., Loeb Classical Library, 1914–1927.

Diodorus of Sicily, 12 vols., Loeb Classical Library, 1933–1967.

HERODOTUS, *The Histories*, trans. A. de Sélincourt, Penguin, rev. edn., 1972.

JOSEPHUS, FLAVIUS, *The Works of Flavius Josephus (The Antiquities of the Jews and The Wars of the Jews)*, trans. W. Whiston, London, 1847; reprinted Grand Rapids, 1960.

PLINY THE ELDER, *Natural History*, 10 vols., Loeb Classical Library, 1938–1962.

PLUTARCH, *Lives*, trans. John Dryden, revised A. H. Clough, New York, 1972 and 1978.

STEPHEN OF BYZANTIUM/STEPHAN VON BYZANZ, *Ethnika*, ed. A. Meineke, reprint, Graz, 1958.

STRABO, *Geography*, 8 vols., Loeb Classical Library, 1917-1932.

THEOPHRASTUS, *Enquiry into Plants*, 2 vols., Loeb Classical Library, 1916 and 1926.

URANIUS, in Stephen of Byzantium.

EARLY TRAVELLERS

BURCKHARDT, J. L., *Travels in Syria and the Holy Land*, London, 1822.

—, *Travels in Arabia*, London, 1829.

CLAYTON, ROBERT (trans.), *A Journal from Grand Cairo to Mount Sinai and Back Again*, London, 1753

DOUGHTY, CHARLES M., *Travels in Arabia Deserta*, 3rd edn., 2 vols., London, 1936.

IRBY, C. L., & MANGLES, J., *Travels in Egypt and Nubia, Syria and Asia Minor*, London, 1823.

LABORDE, LÉON DE, *Journey through Arabia Petraea*, London, 1836.

NIEBUHR, CARSTEN, *Travels in Arabia and other Countries in the East*, 2 vols., Edinburgh, 1792; reprint London, 1994.

POCOCKE, RICHARD, *Description of the East, and some other countries*, 2 vols., London 1743–1745.

MODERN WORKS

AVI-JONAH, M., *The Holy Land: A Historical Geography*, Jerusalem, 1966.

BALL, WARWICK, *Rome in the East*, London and New York, 2000.

BIENKOWSKI, PIOTR (ed.), *Early Edom and Moab: The Beginning of the Iron Age in Southern Jordan*, Sheffield Archaeological Monographs 7, Sheffield, 1992.

BOWERSOCK, G. W., *Roman Arabia*, Cambridge, Mass., 1983.

BRÜNNOW R. E. and DOMASZEWSKI A. VON, *Die Provincia Arabia*, 3 vols., Strasburg, 1904–1909.

CANTINEAU, JEAN, *Le Nabatéen*, 2 vols., Osnabruck, 1978.

COLT, H. D. (ed.), *Excavations at Nessana*, 3 vols., Princeton, 1962.

DINSMOOR, W. B., *The Architecture of Ancient Greece*, New York and London, 1975.

EVENARI, M., *et al.*, *The Negev: The Challenge of a Desert*, Cambridge, Mass., 1971, rev. edn. 1982.

FREND, W. H. C., *The Rise of Christianity*, Philadelphia, 1984.

GLUECK, NELSON, *Rivers in the Desert*, New York, 1959.

—, *Deities and Dolphins*, London, 1965.

—, *The Other Side of the Jordan*, New Haven, 1940; rev. edn. Cambridge, Mass. 1970.

GROOM, NIGEL, *Frankincense and Myrrh*, London and New York, 1981.

HAMMOND, PHILIP, *The Excavation of the Main Theater at Petra, 1961-62*, London, 1965.

—, *The Nabataeans – Their History, Culture and Archaeology*, Studies in Mediterranean Archaeology 37, Gothenburg, 1973.

JAUSSEN, A. and SAVIGNAC, R., *Mission Archéologique en Arabie*, 2 vols., Paris, 1909 and 1914.

JOUKOWSKY, MARTHA SHARP, *Petra Great Temple*, Vol. 1, Providence RI, 1998.

LINDNER, M., *Petra und das Königreich der Nabatäer*, Munich, 5th edn.,1989.

LITTMANN, E., *Semitic Inscriptions: Nabataean Inscriptions from the Southern Hauran*, (Division IV, Section A), Leyden, 1914.

LYTTELTON, M., *Baroque Architecture in Classical Antiquity*, London, 1974.

MCKENZIE, JUDITH, *The Architecture of Petra*, Oxford, 1990.

MESHORER, Y., *Nabataean Coins*, Qedem 3, Jerusalem, 1975.

MILIK, J. T., *Dédicaces faites par les dieux*, Paris, 1972.

MILLAR, FERGUS, *The Roman Near East 31 BC–AD 337*, London and Cambridge, Mass., 1993.

NAVEH, JOSEPH, *Early History of the Alphabet*, Jerusalem, 1982.

NEHMÉ, LAÏLA and VILLENEUVE, FRANÇOIS, *Pétra: Métropole de l'Arabie Antique*, Paris, 1999.

NEGEV, AVRAHAM, *Nabataean Archaeology Today*, New York and London, 1986.

—, *The Architecture of Mampsis*, 2 vols., Qedem 26 and 27. Jerusalem, 1988.

—, *Personal Names in the Nabataean Realm*, Qedem 32, Jerusalem, 1991.

PATRICH, JOSEPH, *The Formation of Nabataean Art*, Jerusalem, 1990.

SHAHID, IRFAN, *Byzantium and the Arabs in the 4th Century*, Dumbarton Oaks, 1984.

—, *Rome and the Arabs*, Dumbarton Oaks, 1984.

—, *Byzantium and the Semitic Orient before the Rise of Islam*, London, 1988.

TEIXIDOR, JAVIER, *The Pagan God*, Princeton, 1977.

TRIMINGHAM, J. S., *Christianity among the Arabs in Pre-Islamic Times*, London and New York, 1979.

WEBER, THOMAS and WENNING, ROBERT (eds.), *Petra: Antike Felsstadt zwischen arabisher Tradition und griechischer Norm*, Mainz, 1997.

WINNETT, F. V., and REED, W. L., *Ancient Records from North Arabia*, Toronto, 1970.

YADIN, Y., *The Finds from the Bar Kokhba Period in the Cave of Letters*, Jerusalem, 1963.

—, *Bar Kokhba*, London and New York, 1971.

ZAYADINE, F. (ed.), *Petra and the Caravan Cities*, Amman, 1990.

INDEX